Mommy? No!!

Mommy? No!!

An Adopted Child's Chronicle of Abuse and Reunification

TONY LADRON DE GUEVARA JR

ISBN: 0615877982
ISBN 13: 9780615877983

Mommy? No! is a true account of a man's journey to connect to his bio-logical mother. Adopted at six-months-old, Tony pulls his audience into the emotional, physical, and psychological abuse he suffered at the hands of his adoptive mother. Tony, a biracial child of Filipino and Caucasian heritage, weaves a revealing saga of a life less lived until he locates his birth mother through the social services mayhem.

Every jaw-dropping page reveals the horrific suffering he endured. We, as readers, see Tony in the beginning in all the innocence of a child. We see childhood lost through his eyes when his adoptive parents reveal to him at five-years-old that he was not their biological child.

Like a skydiver spinning out of control, we are vacuumed emotion-ally and psychologically into his turbulent world as he tries desperately to survive at the often merciless hands of his adopted mother. We, as his audience, suffer along with him.

Warning: You may feel a need to put this book down, rest awhile, and then resume your reading. It is a powerful, compelling story, but requires a firm commitment by the reader to stay with it until the very end; for it is at times emotionally draining. That said; you will keep coming back until you know the whole story.

Few books, based on true accounts, take you on the emotional ride as this book. From start to finish, you, like Tony want to believe it is all a bad dream from which you will eventually awaken. From the get-go you will connect with Tony's life-story. It is riveting, the content often transforming between now-and-then, past-and-present, as his memories flood in-and-out, then surface again for the telling.

Few survivors muster the courage to share the mental anguish they experienced in the midst of an abusive rollercoaster. We are there with Tony as he seemingly rips pages from the stories of his life. It is then; we see clearly the events played out in real-time. As he tells his story we join in his journey to survive, triumph over all diversity, and steadfastly cling to hope.

Eventually, when Tony finds his bio-mother and siblings, his other family, we are witness to a fantastic transformation as he enters a world completely different than the hellhole he's known. It is then, we see him wrapping his mind around the horrible yesterdays he's known at the hands of his adoptive mother, and we watch and listen as he takes us on another emotional journey of hope, renewal, love and acceptance.

Tony is the keeper of his past history, knowing full well, that it continues as he embraces his new family. All the while trying to make sense of the senseless, often life-threatening abuse he suffered at the hands of his adoptive mother.

Tony has a story to tell. It is a real story of deep, heartfelt pain, suffering, and the story of a child clinging to the outstretched arms of hope. He seemingly says to us, *I see all I survey, but who would know me and not know my name?* Always, Tony knows he doesn't fit into the life-hand he was dealt. His search for answers leads him back to the beginning, back to his biological mother, and back into the gift of a mother's unconditional love. This book will grip your heartstrings from beginning to end.

Table of Contents

In Loving Memory of
Marvin Leroy Fredericks

September 22, 1934 – October 29, 2013

ALTHOUGH MARVIN WAS not my father by blood, he was more of a father than a biological son could ask for. He treated me as his own and for this, I am forever grateful. He was a dedicated husband, a loving father, an inspirational relative and a great friend to many.

After finding my biological mother, Marvin was the first person I had the pleasure of speaking with when I made that initial phone call to my mom. My very first impression was this man is a gentle and caring soul. Mom could not have married a better man. After I physically met him, I was right. His generosity, love, and sarcastic but humorous wit shall long be remembered, carried and passed on by all those who knew him.

Marvin transitioned to the next phase of his journey on October 29th, 2013 from cancer. He is missed physically but remains in our hearts spiritually.

Goodbye for now Dad. We'll see you on the other side.

Death leaves a heartache no one can heal, love leaves a memory no one can steal. _ **Irish Headstone**

Acknowledgements

I WANT TO THANK the following people:

-Mr. Sanchez for being the guardian angel when I needed you the most.

-My sister Lisa, who helped me edit this book into the wee hours of the morning and who has also been a cornerstone in our family's foundation.

-My biological mom; Virginia, and my sister Gwyn for allowing me to share our personal stories.

-Eva Moore-Nelson for the many photographs of my nephew to get the cover photo perfect, and for taking hundreds more of our family.

-All Social Workers who are underpaid and overworked who try to make the difference in a child's life.

- Most importantly; Rosa, for being with me all these years through more thick than thin. You have been my pillar of strength.

Dedication

To my beautiful and angelic granddaughter, Savannah, you have taught me the true meaning of unconditional love. You will never go without love, hugs, and kisses; especially from me. If I were put on this earth for a reason, then it is you who I am here for. God has given me another chance to prove I am worthy of a child's love and trust. He has granted me the opportunity to relive the innocent childhood that I never had through you and with you. The story books, sandcastles, and fantasy adventures that we share mean more to me than you can ever imagine. You have changed my perspective about life and are now the focal point and center of my universe.

I cannot keep you from the inevitable heartbreaks you will have in your life, but I will do my best to teach you how to prevent them. I cannot keep you from the inevitable disappointments in life, but I will do my best to teach you how to minimize them. I cannot stop the falls that you will encounter in your life, but I will do my best to catch you when you do. In the end, no matter what happens in your life, I will be there for you; even if I'm at the other end of the world.

Thank you for sharing your snacks and treats with me when you wouldn't share them with anyone else. Thank you for telling me I love you papa when I least expect it. Thank you for those long hugs that you give me when I see you. Thank you for putting your favorite blanket on me when I fell asleep and being really quiet so I wouldn't wake up. Thank you for those long and deep conversations that we have that only a grand-daughter and grandfather can understand. Thank you for teaching me how to dance without caring who is watching. Thank you for reading to me even though you don't know how to read yet. Thank you for inviting me to your tea parties where no boys are allowed except me. Thank you for sprinkling your magic pixie dust on me in my time of need. Most of all, thank you for loving me the way you do.

Foreword

I'LL NEVER FORGET the day my mom confessed her shocking revelation of a secret brother I never knew existed. It was a day that shook my world from its foundation, and forever promised to change my life.

When the phone rang that day, I thought it was going to be just another ordinary phone call from Mom. Except this time, instead of Mom's usual cheerful self, she sounded alarmingly serious. "I have some news for you and your brothers, but I can't tell you over the phone." She gravely announced.

My heart immediately started racing as my mind thought of the worst possible scenarios. I felt like I was going to have a panic attack. Mom had never been the dramatic type. Oh my God, what could be wrong? Was she dying? Did something terrible happen to Dad?

Then as if she sensed my panic, she added, "Don't worry. It's not tragic."

Those words gave me some relief, but what could possibly be so serious that she had to tell us in person?

The next few days filled with worry and stress as I tried to go about my normal routine. Yet, I still imagined the worst and hoped for the best news.

The following weekend, Mom and Dad drove down from Washington. My brothers, James and Tom, and I met them in Maupin, Oregon where Tom was working as a raft guide for the summer.

Mom and Dad sat the three of us down at a picnic table by the Deschutes River. Mom pulled out a large manila envelope while Dad remained silent. She held it tightly against her chest and took a deep breath.

The story began to unravel as she spoke about her past.

"Thirty-five-years ago," she began, "before I met and married your Dad, I became pregnant and gave up a baby boy for adoption. This baby is now an adult. He found me and wants to meet all of us. His name is Tony."

My brothers and I sat in wide-eyed silence, not believing what we'd just heard. Mom, a devout Catholic, was from an extremely religious family, so much so; two of our aunts were nuns. Mom and Dad had been happily married for over thirty years, and I grew up thinking our normal, ordinary family of 5 was one of the most boring families I knew. She was the last person on earth we would have ever expected to deliver a scandalous story of giving birth to a baby out of wedlock.

She pacified our disbelief when she produced an 8X10-inch photo from the envelope she still clasped to her chest. As she pulled the picture from the envelope, time for an instant stopped. She had our full attention as we watched every inch of the photo emerge from its hiding place.

As she turned the photograph toward us, our eyes fixed on the handsome stranger. The man staring back at us had our features: dark hair, brown eyes, and a tan complexion. He looked just like our mother. There was no mistaking that he was indeed related to us. As we looked at the picture, Mom handed us a heartfelt letter Tony had written to us, his siblings.

A month later, we met Tony for the first time. This not only began a new relationship all of us, but it changed how I viewed what was important in my life. Little did any of us know our happy reunion with our new brother had a dark background story all its own. It would be the first of many hidden secrets and eye-opening revelations.

After getting to know Tony, after seeing my mother's life through her eyes, I feel changed for the better. I've learned that things are not always as they appear on the surface. Even the most seemingly "normal" people may carry life altering burdens and secrets. Tony's courage to find his birth-mother mirrors the courage of my mother to come forward with the truth and to possess the fortitude and strength to unite all her children into the happy family we enjoy today.

What you are about to read is Tony's story. Yet, it is our family's story. I am in awe and admiration of my brother, Tony, for triumphing over adversity, and oftentimes working against insurmountable odds to find his birth-mother. His courage and determination in sharing his incredible story with all of us is remarkable. May his perseverance to succeed in life, despite the obstacles inspire you as it has inspired us, and may his story capture your hearts as he has captured ours.

Lisa Fredericks-Chandler (Tony's younger sister).

1

Forgetting to Remember

WHEN IT COMES to memory, the brain is a complex and inconsistent organ. There are things that I can remember years ago as if they happened yesterday. Then there are things that happened last month that I forget altogether. When the Space Shuttle blew up, when 9/11 unfolded in front of me on TV, I remember exactly where and what I was doing in every detail. The common thread seems to be that memories of trauma are stored at the very forefront of my memory storage. For others, traumatic memories are stored at the deepest recesses of the brain to be forgotten forever. I am not as fortunate.

I recall in minute detail the day that I had to put my Chow Chow to sleep years ago. After she was diagnosed with cancer, her quality of life diminished every day for two weeks. She lost her appetite and the tail that always wagged for me when she saw me, no longer wagged. She had to be hand fed and carried outside to use the bathroom.

When I made the decision to let her go, it was the most difficult decision I ever had to make in my life. On the morning I made that decision she could barely lift her head up. I knew it was the best thing to do to stop her from suffering any further.

Arriving at the parking lot of the vet's office, she became excited to be outside and she became lively again. I knew, however, if I took her back home, she would only worsen and suffer even more. It ripped my heart out to see her walk on her own and see her excitement. I second guessed about what I was going to do, but I did not want her to suffer anymore. I carried her into the vet's office where they let me have our last moments together. Despite the pain she felt from the vet inserting the catheter into to her paw, my baby looked up at me with trusting eyes. She knew I wouldn't let any harm come to her. She closed her eyes and then stopped breathing and her head rested gently into my arm. I began to cry like I never cried before.

As I write this, I relive that very moment like it just happened. And so it goes throughout the writing of this book.

Recorded Memories

As children, we reveled in our imaginations as to what we would become when we grew up. I remember some of us wanting to be the President and we came up with serious (of course absurd) laws to give free candy and toys to all the children in the world. Others dreamt about being a fireman, professional athlete, movie star or an astronaut. The common thread seemed to be that most of the kids I knew wanted to become people of stature, fame and/or wealth. Not me. As strange as it may sound, I wanted to become an inanimate object: a new video recorder. This would have the ability to create, play and erase videos. You see, then I would have the ability to rewind myself and then record over whatever memories that I chose to. To this day I still try to aspire to become that recorder. But rather than a new one, I only manage to become a broken, second-hand one. It comes with a rewind button that flips on at will and a record button that won't tape over the old unwanted video.

Music has the uncanny ability to unlock memories stored deep within our minds. We can associate events and people clearly when a certain song plays on the radio, even if that event happened many years ago. With me, certain things that I see day to day trigger those memories. When I see these events, the tape recorder goes on auto-rewind. For example, a child crying, a mom berating her toddler, or a certain painful look a child gives to an adult, brings to the surface those emotions that make my hands sweat or my heart feel as though it's being squeezed through a fine wired meshed net.

Today, however, a re-run of Platoon on HBO puts my thoughts into a time rewind machine. I think back to my life in the year 1968. Incomplete memories, like pieces of a jigsaw puzzle, are very clear but fragmented. I recall a period that my mom and I were living alone in a small two-bedroom apartment in Stockton, California. My (adoptive) dad was enlisted in the Army and completing a second tour in Vietnam. Children like me were referred to as military brats. I was four years old at the time.

REWIND BUTTON: DAD IN GUADALAJARA, MEXICO

The rewind button engages and goes several decades back:

Dad grew up in Guadalajara, Mexico, as the oldest of two sisters and a brother. He was raised in a strict Catholic family. Dad never really talked much about his childhood; in fact, this is all I really know about his childhood years. He came to California illegally, worked odd jobs and sent money back to support his family in Mexico. Eventually, with enough money he was able to bring his family to Los Angeles. Getting his citizenship proved to be difficult and he was only able to do so by enlisting into the Army as a contingency.

My (adoptive) mom was born in Hokkaido, Japan. Her childhood is clearer to me than my own. She would always tell me stories of how World War II had such a devastating effect on her family and how fortunate I was to be born when I was. She was the second oldest of three brothers and two sisters. Her family was poor and had gone many a day without eating because of the lack of money and the rationing of food due to the war. She never had *getas* (Japanese sandals) that matched and her clothes were second-hand and tattered. She and her elder brother were responsible for the welfare of the younger siblings while her father was off fighting the war and her mother was doing what she could to make financial ends meet.

Basic survival was the most important thing in their lives. There was no time for school, but when she was able to attend, she was only met with taunts and belittling from the other children. They would refer to her and her siblings as *kojiki-n-ko* literally child *of the poor*. When literally translated to English, it does not sound so bad, however in Japanese it is regarded as a supreme insult.

She would always remind me how lucky I was to have food, clothes, shelter and an education. These were luxury items that she could not have as a child. If I left even a single grain of rice in my bowl, she would constantly remind me of the day she picked out a grain of rice from a toilet and washed it off so that she could have nourishment. Rice, while she was growing up was extremely rationed and was strictly for the soldiers or the rich.

My adoptive father met my adoptive mother while he was stationed in Japan. They fell in love and soon thereafter married. After completing a tour in Japan, Dad was assigned to the Sacramento Army Depot in California in 1963.

After unsuccessful attempts to bear a child, Mom went through extensive tests and surgery to find answers for her inability to conceive. The doctors found scar tissues and badly damaged, unrepairable fallopian tubes. Consequently, conception was not an option.

Several years later, I would understand how her tubes became physically damaged and she became emotionally scarred.

The following year, Mom and Dad decided to adopt a child. They chose The *Children's Home Society* in Sacramento to assist them in finding an infant that was available for adoption. The adoption process was, from what I was told by Mom, complicated and expensive.

Fast forward four years. Dad received orders to go to Vietnam. While he was there, Mom attended night classes to learn to read and write English.

The only way of successfully communicating with Dad overseas was to use a reel-to-reel tape deck. Mom and I would sit on the floor of her bedroom listening to a tape of my father's voice. It was a tough time for both of us. We could hear the stress and loneliness in his voice. Oftentimes, we could even hear the distant sound of gunfire, explosions and other sounds of war. Other times the tape would cut off, inexplicably, in mid-sentence. When Dad continued recording, he never explained why or what caused the tape to cut off. I'm sure he didn't elaborate so we wouldn't worry any more than we already were.

Aside from the fragments of memories that I do have, other memories I have prior to five-years-old are relegated to old homemade 8mm film movies and faded childhood pictures. From this, it seemed I had a pretty normal and happy childhood. Mom looked like she was giving, loving and caring. She was always smiling in the pictures and homemade movies. She never seemed too far away from me. She appeared very protective and nurturing. From an outsider's perspective, this could not be a woman that would ever harm her child. But, that became the furthest thing from the truth.

THE ABUSE BEGINS

The physical and emotional abuse started prior to the time I was in Kindergarten. I was around five-years-old. I can remember it clearly because it was shortly after my parents decided to tell me that I was adopted. My father had returned from Vietnam and was able to get an assignment back to Japan. We were now based in Sagamihara, Japan.

It was later in the evening after dinner. We were involved in our usual routine of sitting around our small thirteen-inch, black and white TV and watching Japanese movies. As usual, the rabbit ear antennae had to be constantly maneuvered to get clear reception when the channels were changed. There were no remote

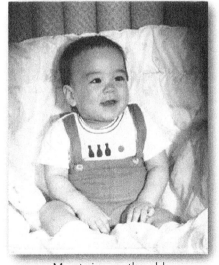

Me at six-months-old

controls in those days. I *was* the remote control. Since the TV was so small, I'd sit only a foot or two away. When it was time to change the channel, I was given the verbal command, *Change the channel*. That was high technology in the 60's.

On this night the feeling was somewhat somber. I could feel the mood in the house was unusually quiet. My mom and dad came from the bedroom and shut off the TV and asked me to sit on the sofa. It was an old oversized sofa that my dad would always sit on after work. As a matter of respect, I knew never to sit on it while he was home. It was his throne, but that night I was told to sit on it. My parents sat in front of me and I could tell from their expressions that what they were about to tell me was not going to be comfortable.

I don't recall the exact words that night. I do know they wanted me to understand that they loved me and that no matter what; I was still their child. The exact details of what was said seem hazed in obscurity. What I do recall was how I felt. I couldn't quite grasp this concept of not actually being their physical child. After all, these were the only parents that I had ever known. There was this immediate sense of rejection and confusion. In an instant I was now thrust into a world of detachment. I was now an outsider connected only by an umbilical cord of paper court documents. They showed me official looking paperwork so I would be convinced that this was not some sort of scheme devised by the boogieman. However, no boogieman was scarier than what I was feeling at that point. I cried. I cried for a very long time.

In hindsight, that night seemed like I was twisting and turning inside of a tornado, like Dorothy in The Wizard of Oz. Thoughts in my head were just twisting and turning and spinning. At five years old, all I can remember feeling was confusion. I couldn't quite comprehend what was being told to me. Adopted? How does a mom just give her child away? It seemed strange that a mom could do that. And why would *this* mom decide to have me instead? So many questions kept jostling around in my head. Even when Mom and Dad tried their best to explain it, I couldn't really understand it. *This* was my mom and dad! How could I have another?

The couch I sat in felt so much bigger, as if it were swallowing me. I felt smaller than small. My whole life seemed to have an altered meaning from that point on. I was too young to understand it then. I just knew that what I felt at that moment was not a good thing. As much as they both attempted to tell me how much they loved me and that I was their child regardless of the circumstances, I knew that I wasn't. And, even though I knew nothing of my real mother, I felt an overwhelming feeling of being thrown away.

From that point on, inwardly, I felt different. Looking back, there was an emptiness deep inside of me, which would propagate as the years went on. But at that time, I was too young to let it consciously bother me. It wasn't important since I was only five years old. There were too many swings to swing on and slides to slide down. Life for me was fun and filled with sandboxes. At least, so I thought.

I don't think I changed outwardly. I was still an innocent child with the world as my playground. No, it wasn't me. It was my mom that began to change. The change seemed to occur in a single night. It was as though by telling me this dark secret, she somehow morphed into a different person. This is as far back as I can remember when the abuse began.

The punishments never seemed to fit the crime, but during that time I didn't know this. Not eating my vegetables led to open handed slaps to the face. Those same vegetables would then find their way to my breakfast plate. (There's something about cheerios and cold spinach that doesn't blend well. Even on St Patrick's Day, green tinted milk is not appetizing.)

I also had a tendency to be a slow eater. This irked my mom to an extreme degree and reaching across the table to slap me evidently became too taxing for her. One night, while I approached the dinner table, I noticed we had a new centerpiece. It was a bowl of fake plastic fruit consisting of an apple, pear, orange, grapes and a banana that sat at the top of this synthetic heap. It was an eyesore (and to this day, still is).

Rather than having to reach clear across the table to slap me, she would reach for the banana and hit me upside my head. Although it was plastic, the very tip of the banana was hard as a rock. At the end of the night, I would end up with multiple knots on the top of my head. As funny as that vision looks to me now, I recall the blinding pain and almost choking on my food as I gasped for air as I cried.

At one point, I couldn't take it anymore and I became quicker than she. As soon as I saw her reach for the banana, I'd quickly drop to the floor underneath the dining room table. I would try to cover my head with my arms but that just caused her to become angrier. She would then just kick me until I came back up and then hit me more.

To me emotional abuse leaves deeper scars than physical abuse. While both leave scars, the emotional scars can fester and never heal. The pain of having hairs ripped by the roots from my scalp would eventually go away. The searing pain and stinging from an open-handed slap to my face would slowly dissipate. The loneliness of being shut into a dark room with no lights and no dinner would be circumvented when the morning sun came up. However, the deepest scar and the worst pain of all, was not understanding why my mom no longer loved me. She had never done this to me before. She looked at me with such hatred and repugnancy. What did I do to make her hate me all of a sudden? What did I do that was so wrong? God, I was only five.

One of the emotional scars that still plays like a broken record is the humiliation I was put through in front of my neighborhood friends. After playing outside until dusk my mom would yell for me to come in the house. Immediately I would see the look of fear in the eyes of my play buddy's eyes. I would have faced any type of physical pain than go through what she was about to put me through.

Grass stains and dirt on my coveralls was not tolerated. If I came home with any of these on my clothes, I would be punished. These punishments came in the form of multiple slaps to my face or head. Mom would then tear all my clothes off and drag me to the front door. I would scream and beg not to be put outside. This plea always was ignored. She would propel me with such force that I would clear the porch and end up in the walkway. I would then run back and flatten myself as close as possible to the door so that I could be sandwiched between the screen and main door.

Through the crack in the door, I would plead with my mom. "Mommy?"

"No!!"

"Please let me in. Please, don't do this to me. Please let me in the house!"

Time seemed infinite. I was now a circus sideshow freak. The military housing area was shaped in squared horseshoe fashion. The middle area was a large grassy field speckled with a few trees. This is where the neighborhood children would gather together to play. Even though I could be seen by the world, I imagined that the screen door was solid. I would sob silently to myself in the hope that no one would hear or see me. I never looked behind me to see who was watching but I knew all the neighborhood kids were there. I could hear them giggling and making jokes. I would just keep my head in the corner of the doorway and continued to beg my mom to let me in through the crack door. I imagined myself to be smallest bug in the world.

Mom eventually realized that the screen door wasn't allowing for my full humiliation. Like a farmer holding a squawking chicken, she would take me by the back of my neck and then hold me in place on the porch. My crying and screaming would then attract my friends and anyone else to watch. She made sure she held me so I was forced to look at everyone who was watching. I would just close my eyes and then wish them all away. If I couldn't see them, then they couldn't see me.

Minutes seemed like hours. As darkness fell, the kids would go home to dinner. At that point, there would be no reason to keep me outside and I was allowed to come in, only to be told to go to my room without dinner and shut the lights off. If dinner was allowed, it had already been sitting out for hours where it became cold, bland, and tasteless. I would eat what I could, only to find what I didn't eat would still be on the table for the next day for breakfast.

Beatings and slapping's from my mom became routine. It never occurred to me that this wasn't normal. In fact, I accepted it because it was all I knew. I thought all children were beaten like this. I had nothing to compare it to since I had no brothers or sisters. I dared not talk about it outside of the house. During my beat downs, it was verbally driven in to me that 'it was nobody's business what was done within our family'. As such, I never told anyone. The fear of what would be done to me, if I did, was insurmountable. It was our family secret.

When I turned six, the beatings were now combined with verbal assaults. I would be repetitively reminded that I was adopted.

"Nobody wanted you. We felt sorry for your ass! I didn't want a boy! I wanted a girl so bad! Your father wanted a boy to carry on the last name!"

Those words penetrated deeply. The small hole inside of me became bigger with time. The word 'rejection' does not explain the emptiness a six-year-old can feel when told such things. These words still echo through my mind to this very day. As much as I want to forget, it seems to be imprinted into my core forever.

After being told this, I literally wanted to die. I felt like a burden - a waste to my mom and no longer wanted to exist. I was predestined to be a disappointment no matter what I did. I couldn't change my gender so I could do no right. The next day, I grabbed some plastic clothesline and went to the middle of the housing area. How appropriate it seemed that among all the trees, this particular tree stood alone. It was different as though it, too, was separated and cast out from the rest. I reached for the lowest branch and tied the clothesline around it. Fashioning a crude noose from a slipknot I looped the remaining clothesline around my neck. Bending my legs and letting my weight fall forward, the clothesline, made of plastic, stretched with my weight and I fell to my knees. I couldn't even get this right.

I contemplate this scenario now -suicidal thoughts at six-years-old? What could be so bad that a child of six would want to end their life? How I felt emotionally far outweighed the beatings that I endured. If there was a God and an afterlife, then I no longer wanted to be part of this world. Bad became worse, and more suicide attempts followed later in my childhood.

As time went on, my feelings of abandonment became more and more prevalent. I dreaded the weekends. Mom and Dad were young and liked to drink and party. Their routine was to put me to bed early and wait until I fell asleep. They would close my door and get themselves ready to go out. When they believed I was fast asleep, they would tiptoe out to the club for a night of drinking and dancing. I didn't know this at first. My first experience in finding no one at home late at night was traumatic. I remember waking up from a nightmare and screaming for my mom. No one came to rescue me in the darkness of my room. My only solace was the faint sound of the stereo coming from the living room.

I ran from the bedroom and frantically searched for them, but the house was empty. I felt so alone and empty. It was my first feeling of helplessness and physical abandonment. I went to my parents' room. It was the only room where I could find some comfort and consolation. I could still smell my mom's perfume and my dad's Hai Karate cologne. I wanted to stay in there until they returned, but Mom would only be angry with me. I resigned myself back to my room and sat up in bed crying and rocking back and forth until I fell back asleep.

After that night, I was now aware of the weekend ritual. The stereo would always be left playing to make me think they were home. I was able to recognize the sounds of my mom's high heels clicking as she walked down the hallway. I hated that sound. It meant that soon they would be gone. One night I wanted to be as close to my mom as I could without her knowing. Walking quietly to my bedroom door, I would lie on my side and peek underneath the crack of the door. I could see my mom's reflection from the shiny, waxed, hardwood floor. As she walked by my room, her perfume would waft downwards through the door. She always smelled nice and looked so pretty.

When the front door of the house would open, slowly and quietly, I would start to repeat the words 'please don't go' quietly over and over. When the sound of the deadbolt echoed through the house, I would plead in a louder voice:

"Please come back, please come back! Please?"

Still peering underneath the door, I would fall asleep on my side lying on the floor until they came home. I would then quickly run to my bed, relieved that they were now home. I always feared that one day they would not return. These events, and being placed for adoption, became the foundation to my abandonment issues and attachment disorder later in my life.

Later that year we visited my relatives on my mom's side. My aunt was 19 and was living at home with my grandparents. She was going through a rebellious stage at this point in her life and was constantly fighting with them. One night, I went up to her room after she had big fallout with my mom and grandparents. She was crying so I went upstairs to try to console her. I knew what it felt like to be alienated and thought I could help make her pain go away.

She was kneeling with her face in her hands sobbing. I walked up to her and placed my arms around her neck and hugged her for a long time. She hugged me back. Then unexpectedly, she kissed me on the mouth and took my hand and placed it on her breast. I didn't know what to do so she showed me how she wanted me to touch her. I did so and then ran to my room.

When I recall this, I don't recall it with any negative feelings that I had at that time. She approved of what I did and this was just another form of positive validation for me. I didn't think it was wrong. I brought happiness to someone who was older and who I respected. Nothing ever happened after that. However, I now understand how a child may not understand that being touched inappropriately is wrong. Could this be why some child victims of sexual abuse seldom report this type of abuse? When a child is punished with physical abuse but rewarded or validated after sexual abuse, does the understanding of what is right and what is wrong become occluded? I am sure that there is also the fear that no one would believe the child and be further punished for lying. I am not a psychologist; therefore I can only speak to how I feel.

Although there were many other opportunities for my aunt to see me after this incident, she never did. Perhaps the guilt of what she had done prevailed and she felt ashamed. I will never know.

My memories of this time period stop here. The recorder stops. I push the fast forward button and it stops when I turned eight years old.

Third Grade Parent – Role Reversal

My father was now assigned to the Los Angeles Recruiting Command. As a military recruiter, he would spend long hours away from home. We would only see him a couple of hours at night and working weekends were the norm for him. He had monthly quotas to meet and when they were not met, it made for longer hours at the office.

My mother decided to take a job at this point. I became a latchkey kid. It was a double-edged sword. Although it meant a couple of hours of total freedom, that freedom came with complete seclusion and adult responsibilities. I wasn't allowed to go to the playground or visit with my friends. Mom would make a list of chores for me to accomplish before she got home. This included cleaning the house and preparing the evening meal for the family. As usual, if things were not done to her liking, it would be conveyed to me through a barrage of insults or face slaps.

Our main staple was white rice. It had to be rinsed several times to wash out the starch and the right amount of water had to be added in order for it to get the right consistency. Too much water would cause the rice to be too soft and mushy. Not enough water and the rice would be too hard. I learned the hard way to figure out exactly how much water was needed to get the perfect consistency, but it came at a physical price. Through trial and error and enough slaps to my head, I found that the water level shouldn't exceed the first line of my first finger when touching the bottom of the pot. The fear of not preparing the perfect dinner weighed heavily on me. Heaven forbid that I under or overcooked something. That was simply an automatic beat down.

At eight years old, one would think that the most I would have to worry about was whether or not there was sand in my shoes from the playground or if the street lights were about to come on because it was getting late.

I was told that although I was being beaten, it was a form of attention. Mom said that the day the beatings stopped is the day that they no longer cared or no longer loved me. It seemed to make logical sense that if someone no longer cared for the other, no effort would be made on that person's behalf. So the beatings equated to love. I actually started to believe it.

I never asked about my adoption after that fateful night when I was five. Again, Mom said it was nobody's business. Now that I was a little older, Mom felt I had a better understanding of life circumstances. She explained that my biological mother and father were foreign exchange students at a university in Sacramento. The adoption agency told her that my birth mom was of Indonesian descent and my father was Germanic. I was given up for adoption at birth and stayed in an orphanage until my adoptive parents went through the 'legal hassles' of my adoption.

This story was constantly repeated, emphasis placed on the 'hassles' they had to endure. I didn't like being considered a 'hassle'. It's as if I wasn't worth the effort and they had so many more important things to do. I was just a nuisance to be added to their already busy schedule, but I was lucky enough that they could fit me in.

Whenever my mom would beat me, she would always conclude the event with wanting to know if I now wanted to find my 'real mother'. Despite the constant reminder that I was an unwanted adopted child, I still felt that these were my only parents. It was like she wanted me to admit that I did, indeed, feel like an unwanted stepchild. I believe that in her thinking, this would exonerate her of her abuse of me.

Mom had a thing about beating me on the head and face. It was like she wanted to disfigure my face or something. Consequently, I started to suffer from nosebleeds. I wouldn't just bleed for a short time or just trickles. It was profuse. Blood would just flow like a water faucet. It got everywhere. At first, mom was a little concerned. The nosebleeds became consistent. It got to the point that I would bleed without much effort from my mom's head slaps.

Mom was now convinced that I was just willing myself to bleed on purpose so she wouldn't hit me anymore. I wonder if this was some psychosomatic manifestation that gave credence to Mom's theory. The power of words on a child are immeasurable. To this day, I actually believe what she said was true.

The nosebleeds no longer deterred her from beating me. In fact, it made her even angrier that I was getting blood on things she would have to wash. I started to get sick from all the blood I ingested. I could feel the blood clots form in my nose, and then extend down the back of my throat. It caused a gag reflex and I often found myself hugging the toilet bowl to throw up all the blood that accumulated in my stomach.

2

A New Chapter in My Life

THIS TIME PERIOD began a new chapter in my life. The focus of attention now turned to Mom. As a child, I did not understand alcoholism. Again, I thought every family experienced what I was experiencing. It was just another family secret. As Dad spent less and less time at home, Mom started sending me to the liquor store with a note giving me permission to buy cigarettes and beer for her. She was a frequent customer and they knew I was her son. Mom's drinking became incessant. I was no longer

the focus of her hatred. My father was now the victim. Mom would accuse Dad of sleeping around and blamed this for his late night returns. She would scream, curse, and throw things at my dad. He wouldn't say anything. He just took it.

Dad wouldn't do anything to hurt Mom. He would avoid confrontation by simply getting into his car and driving away. The next morning Mom would send me out to look for him. He would only be a couple of blocks away sleeping in the driver's seat. I felt sad for him and wished there was something grown up I could say to him. I could only just tap on the car window and tell him that Mom wants him to come home. I don't know how Dad put up with her, but he did and, to my knowledge, still does.

In looking back, I have to respect my father for that. When he was younger, he used to be a boxer. He was stocky and I always knew he was very powerful. Had he lifted a hand to her, I knew he would have killed her. I'm sure he knew it too.

There were many nights that the neighborhood was filled with sirens and lights blaring. One night an ambulance showed up. When I peered into the living room, there was blood on my dad's favorite leather recliner. I didn't know what had happened. I fell asleep despite the sounds of dishes breaking and glass shattering. My mom had come back into the house after talking to the police and bragging that she had put a hole in my dad's head with her high-heeled shoe. She had told the police it was in self-defense, but I knew better.

I missed a lot school during those days. They were spent cleaning up the house while my mom lay in bed sick and hung-over. She would call for me to bring her a bucket to throw up in or bring her a cold towel for her forehead. The bedroom was always cold, dank, and smelled of alcohol and vomit. It was my job to clean it all up. It became a regular weekend binge. I took and I took on the role of the parent and kept telling her that she shouldn't drink so much. It was the only time in my life that I wasn't hit for what she may have construed as talking back.

As a result of these binges, I regularly missed schools on Mondays and sometimes on Fridays if she started drinking early. I hated missing school. It was my sanctuary. Here I received all my validation for anything I did well. When I was in the fifth grade, I developed a crush on my teacher, Ms. Ferges. She had the prettiest smile and the longest blonde hair. Her blue eyes seemed to twinkle at me every time I did something exceptional. I would stay after school to help her carry her books to her car. I wanted so much to impress her and it made me want to do really well in class. Unbeknownst to her, she set the tone of how I would approach life and the successes that came with it. I address this at the end of the book.

Spelling and reading were my strengths. I loved to read. It was my escape from reality. Books could take me to faraway lands of mystical dragons, brave knights and scary trolls. But my true talent, I found, was being in the public eye. Our school was going to put on the annual Christmas play and I volunteered to recite a Christmas poem solo. I put everything I had into memorizing that poem. I knew it would make my teacher happy.

> *There once was a little angel*
> *Who lived on a Christmas tree*
> *But she was not angelic*
> *As angels ought to be*
> *She kicked her little heels up*
> *And waved her arms in the air,*
> *And wore her halo crooked*
> *Upon her golden hair*
> *What's more she didn't care!*[1]...

On my big night, I remember taking center stage and looking out in the audience. I was scared, but confident. I recited the poem word for word. At the end I received a standing ovation and never wanted that feeling of recognition to go away. It set the stage for all the events to come in my life that required me being in front of a crowd or audience. It was one of the few times that Mom looked as though she was proud of me. Yet, even then, she was quick to criticize me for reciting the poem too fast.

As an only child, play activities were limited to doing things that didn't require more than one person. Since none of my friends lived nearby, I had to find a new escape. I started collecting baseball cards. It was something that I could control and have total reign over. I had hundreds of them and would spend hours alphabetizing them and keeping a log of them in a spiral-bound notebook. It took months to get them all organized. I was meticulous. I kept them in 7-Up boxes that were sliced in half

---

1 There was more to this poem but I am unable to recall the rest of it.

lengthwise. This was one of the very few things I could do without having someone to play with. I completely absorbed myself into this hobby. I could shut out everything and imagine myself as a professional baseball player. I wanted to be famous and have millions of fans adoring me. I dreamt that one day I would be famous and adored.

Then one night, my mom walked into my bedroom.

"What in the fuck are you doing? Is that all you give a shit about is your goddamn baseball cards!? Here's what I think about your stupid baseball cards!"

She picked up the box and threw them into the air and walked out. There was no rhyme or reason to what she did or why. She just did it. I just sat there and looked at what took me months to organize. I picked them up one by one and began to feel what true hatred was all about.

Runaway To Adoption Agency

With my lunch, Mom would occasionally give me 50 cents for milk. On the way to school, I would take a slight detour through a back alley to double back to Mr. B's liquor store (the very same place that I would buy Mom's beer and cigarettes). On the bottom shelf of the candy rack there was a bubble gum brand called 'Big Daddy Bubble Gum'. It came in a round long stick about a foot long and came in mouth-watering flavors of watermelon, cherry, apple, and grape. I would buy ten sticks, save two for myself and then sell the other eight for ten cents. That profit was used to buy more products. Short of a briefcase and tie, I became a (very young) business man.

I would take my profit and put it into a small plastic safe. Then, I would hide the safe way in the back on my toy closet. I knew Mom would not approve of what I did with my milk money. Luckily, Mom would be at work so I had enough time to count my loot and then stash my plunder away before she came home.

One night, while hiding underneath the bed cover with a flashlight and my favorite comic book, Mom came into my room. I couldn't turn my flashlight off in time and before I knew it, the covers were ripped from my bed.

"What in the hell are you doing!?"

"Nn-n-nothing Mom..."

"Why in the hell are your teeth green!?"

She made me open my mouth and had me pull out a golf ball sized wad of green apple Big Daddy Bubble gum.

"Where did you get this?"

"Uh...I-I don't know."

Bruce Lee had nothing on the speed of my Mom's fists of fury.

"Don't you ever lie to me! Do you understand? Don't you ever, ever lie to me again!"

Each word was followed by a punch to my head or other uncovered part of my body. Even then, I couldn't tell her that I was using my milk money. It would only mean a worse beating than the last.

"My friend gave it to me!"

She was relentless. After she tired from cursing and hitting me, I curled up and felt the bumps on my head. There were bumps on top of bumps. I fell asleep dreaming that I was Spiderman and would shoot a gob of web around her and hang her from the ceiling until she said she was sorry.

The next day my world came crashing down. Apparently, Mom had been going through my closet where she stored an old travel trunk. In it, she stored her prized kimonos that were handed down to her through her family. On top of that trunk, she found my little plastic safe that hid all my profits. After breaking it open and viewing its content, she beat me senseless.

When she left, I snuck out to the garage and grabbed my skateboard. It was a wooden 'Black Knight ™', with clay wheels but it was my transportation to freedom. I didn't think of anything else other than to get away; far away. I skated fast and hard, weaving in and out of back streets in case she would start looking for me. As I got further away, a feeling of complete freedom and relief came over me. It was exhilarating! She couldn't touch me; my destiny was now in my own hands. I was free! As I skated, I kept looking behind me in case she was trying to find me. The fear of her finding me and taking me back home to beat me, made me skate even harder. I started to devise a plan.

I remember that Sacramento didn't look too far away from Hawthorne on the map. I could simply just head to Redondo Beach, make a right and head north! When I got to Sacramento, I would find the adoption agency from where I came, and they could take me back! This would be a great journey of freedom and a new lease on life. 'Brilliant! What a master plan; why didn't I think of this before?' I thought to myself.

When I got to Fisherman's' Wharf, the smells of the ocean and the wafting odors of grilled fish and boiled crab reminded me that I had this small challenge called hunger. Milling about this place was not a good idea, so I started down the bike path due north and continued my trek. Along the way I found a plastic kite hanging off a tree. Apparently it got away from some poor kid that couldn't keep it under control. I rescued it from where it was. It wasn't your run of the mill, everyday basic kite. It was a blue triangular bat shaped kite, with yellow flaps on the underside where the string would be tethered. It was way cool and since I never had a kite, this one would be a keeper.

Eventually the bike path became a sidewalk and I found myself skating down a residential sidewalk with my new found kite in Manhattan Beach. This was ritzy neighborhood lined with Porsches, BMWs, and Mercedes Benz. One day, I would have one of those. In the meantime, I fantasized that some rich lady would see me and feel sorry for me. I would tell her my story of my wicked mother, and then she would take me to her beach home and adopt me. How grand would that be? Alas, my hunger burst that thought bubble and my belly was aching for some nourishment. I passed a liquor store and I noticed there was a deli inside. I doubled back and went inside.

There was a meat section where one could just get any of the various pre-packed luncheon meats. I had (and still have) a thing for salami and there in front of me was a big ol' honkin' roll of it! I swiftly picked it up and put it under my shirt and held it in place with my arm and using the kite to cover the huge bulge under my arm. I approached the counter to assess the clerk's face to see if he had a clue to what I was doing. To my benefit he was too busy helping a customer to even take notice as I walked out the door. As soon as my wheels were on the ground, I was like a bottle rocket out of control! I skated like my life depended on it. When I got about a hundred yards away, I finally looked back to see if anyone was following. I was in the clear. I immediately sat down on the curb and chowed down! Good thing for garden water faucets, I was pretty thirsty after eating all that salt!

I had made pretty good headway at this point and decided to take a break and enjoy the sand and the beach. With a full belly and warm beach, I made a soft sand pillow and dozed off. This feeling of being independent and free was a feeling unlike any other. For the first time in my short life, I was happy, content, and in control.

When I woke up, the coastal fog began to roll in and it was getting cold. I hopped back on my skateboard to continue my journey but more importantly to warm myself up. In an hour or so, it would start to get dark and the beach city chill was not something I had obviously planned for. The route I was taking was a familiar one. Coming to the beaches on the weekend was a family event so I didn't feel out of my element. That is, until I came to the end of the road at El Segundo beach. I had never gone any further than this and where the bike path was supposed to go north as I hoped, it started veering back east. In front of me was a harbor inlet where boats would go in and of. I was now in Marina Del Rey which led into Santa Monica. The friendly sandy coastline and bike paths now disappeared into a big city metropolis. I had not planned on this! Where was Sacramento? I was now 21 miles away from home and still had 365 miles to go! I had no idea.

Fear was now setting in. This was unknown territory and I didn't want to venture into a big city. Maybe I could swim the channel? No, that's too far. What do I do? My fear seemed to increase with the enveloping night sky. Where would I sleep? How would I stay warm? Why didn't I think about all these things before I left? Grudgingly, I turned about slowly and skated back home. It was the longest and saddest skateboard ride of my life.

When I got back to Hawthorne, I came up with another brilliant   plan. I could go to my buddy Steve's house, and I could live there! I could hide under his bed when his parents were home and come out when they went to work! I should have thought of that before trying to run away to Sacramento! There was still hope of not ever having to be beat again. I knocked on his door and his older brother answered.

'Are you Tony?'

I had never met him before and wondered how he knew my name. 'Yea, is Steve here?' I replied.

He told me to come in while he got his little brother.

'Hey man, everyone is looking for you! Where did you go? The cops were just here and are out searching for you!'

My heart sank; I was out of brilliant plans. Now I had no choice but to go home. I asked Steve not to tell anyone I was there, but before I could explain where I had gone and why, I could see the flashing police lights reflecting into the living room.

The police officer came to the door and asked me if I was okay. I told him I was fine. When he asked me where I went, I told him I was trying to go back to the adoption agency where I had come from and that my parents needed to get their refund. He unsuccessfully tried to stifle his laugh and said 'They are worried about you.' I found that hard to believe.

When I got to the house, I expected the usual look of disappointment and the inevitable beating that was to come. I got neither. Dad looked happy but tired and Mom looked relieved to see me. She asked me if I was hungry and I told her no. She told me to shower and go sleep and then turned her attention to the police officer. I don't know what was said, but we didn't talk about that incident afterwards. The abuse stopped for a while, but it was short lived.

THE HAMSTER THROW

While we lived in Hawthorne, I had hamsters for pets. I kept them in a small glass aquarium and I'd watch them for hours. They ran inside their running wheels or climb through their tubes or curled up with each other while they slept.

However, there was one that stood out from the rest. I named him *Hammie* since he was the ham of the group and what better name could there be for a hamster? He had the coolest brown and white markings and was always scurrying around the cage. I'd always take him out of the cage and play with him on my bed. Soon afterwards, he became determined to get out of the cage. That taste of freedom became his demise.

Three hamsters soon became a dozen and eventually there were just too many to keep. I was told to give them away and I'd be able to only keep one. Of course, I kept Hammie. Since he had no one to play with, I spent more and more time with him by letting him hang out on my desk while I did my homework or played with my plastic Army men. Whenever I tried to put him back into his cage, he'd climb on the wheel or watering tube to try to get out. He just wanted to be out and free. I knew that feeling. I, like Hammie, just wanted to escape to another world and be happy without any worries. I wanted someone to care for me like I cared for Hammie. I felt like I was his protector. Since I couldn't have my fantasy, I lived vicariously through him.

It was just a matter of time before Hammie found his way out of the cage. He'd climb up the watering tube and once he reached the top of his glass house, he would simply hop out. He would then go about the house like a curious cat and find warm places to snuggle into like an old sock or shoe or roamed about as he pleased.

His little hamster droppings, however, were not cute with Mom and she had a conniption fit every time he got out. When he did, I ended up paying the physical price with a beating and/or cursing. She'd threaten to throw him away if I didn't maintain control of him. She would then argue with my dad about '*his* irresponsible son' and *my* out of control pet.

One late night, while I slept, I heard yelling and cursing coming from the living room. Hammie had gotten loose again and Mom was on a rampage. She came into my room and screamed; 'You better find that fucking hamster, or I'm going to kill it!'

I shot out of bed and frantically started looking in all his favorite hiding spots. My dad was looking too and he definitely was not happy about this situation. I kept calling Hammie's name. I didn't care what she was going to do to me; I was in tears over what she was going to do to Hammie. While searching in the spare bedroom, from the living room I heard my dad yell, *Goddammit! Goddamn fucking hamster!*

I ran into the living room and looked in the direction where he was looking. In the bottom side of his favorite leather recliner was a small gnawed out hole that Hammie had made. My dad picked up the recliner with one hand and flipped it onto its side. Out tumbled Hammie. Before I could get to him, Dad picked him up and ran to the front door.

ABSOLUTE FEAR

"Dad! No, please don't! Noooooooooo! Oh my God, no Dad!"

He wound up his arm like an outfielder throwing a baseball to home plate. He threw Hammie as hard and as far as he possibly could. It was dark and I couldn't see where he went. I just crumbled to my knees and cried. The pain of what I just witnessed was incredible. My heart, my body, and my soul hurt so badly.

After a couple of minutes, I managed to get myself up and run to where I thought Hammie would be, but it was dark and I couldn't see anything. The force and velocity alone would have killed Hammie on impact, but I still looked for him until I heard my mom say, *Get in the house right now! Even if it's alive, it's not coming back into this house!*

She was right. If he did survive, he'd have a better chance of surviving outside than coming back into the hell house.

One day, Mom told me to ride my bike to my dad's work to give him the checkbook. She told me to make sure that he got it no matter what. I wasn't to stop anywhere or do anything other than get that checkbook to him. The bike ride would take me about half an hour and Mom told me to get there as quickly as I could. I knew if I didn't, there'd be hell to pay.

I peddled as hard and as fast as I could. I rode on the right side of the street and as close to the curb as possible to keep enough distance between me and the cars driving behind me. I noticed a parked car that was coming up and as I got closer, I looked behind me to see if I'd have enough room. As I did, a car behind me was barreling down the road at a high rate of speed. I didn't think there'd be enough room to squeeze between the passing car and the parked one. It was too late to stop and I hit the back of the parked car at full speed. The impact knocked me unconscious. Helmets were not the law at the time.

When I came to, there were a number of people around me trying to administer first aid. I could feel a huge knot on top of my head and I was feeling nauseous. I looked at my bike as some man was trying to bend the handlebars back into place. The ambulance arrived and all I could hear in my head was, *get this checkbook to your dad as quickly as possible, no matter what!* I didn't know how much time had passed, but I knew I was overdue at dad's office. I was getting scared and feared the inescapable beating that was to come if I didn't hurry.

When the ambulance arrived, the paramedic was trying to put a big plastic collar around my neck and I refused. I told him that I was alright. He said something about a possible concussion and all I could think of was the actual one I was going to get if I didn't hightail it out of there asap.

I barely managed to get up and stagger to my bike. Everyone was trying to convince me to go to the hospital, but I kept refusing. They had no idea the types of worse injuries I would get if I didn't get that checkbook to my dad.

When I got to my dad, he looked surprised to see me, but happy. I gave him the paper bag containing the checkbook. I accomplished the mission! I wasn't going to get the beating I was dreading.

When I got home, I ran to the bathroom and threw up. I felt dizzy and really, really sick. It was about 6:00 p.m., and I went to bed. I didn't wake up until the next day. From my medical training as an adult, all indicators pointed to a pretty bad concussion. The concussion, however, would not have been as bad as what Mom would have dealt me.

MOM'S METHODS OF PUNISHMENT

I don't know where Mom thought up her punishments. I can only specu-late that they were identical or variations of what she went through as a child.

One of her punishments consisted of having me remove all my clothes and forcing me into a kneeling position with my body in a 90-degree angle at the knees. If I broke the angle, I would be whipped with a belt to my back or buttocks. Additionally, I had to hold my arms and hands straight over my head and was not allowed to lower them. If I did, more time was added to my punishment. I knelt in the dark hallway in front of my room until she felt I paid penance. This routinely would be two to three hours. I would have rather endured the pain of a belt lashing than this medieval dungeon torture.

Mom would always justify her punishments by telling me that I was lucky I wasn't born during her generation. She would tell me that her punishments were a hundred times worse than what she put me through.

One day, she actually tried to convince my dad to tie a rope to the ga-rage rafters so I could be punished like she was as a child; hanging upside down by the ankles. Luckily for me, Dad was able to convince her that the beams would not hold my weight. Instead I was relegated to sleeping on the garage floor with my dog.

I spent many nights in the garage sleeping with my dog, Bobby. He would curl up with me while we shared his stinky, blue doggy blanket. He always knew when something was wrong and would do his best to console me. Even my dog was scared of mom. He wasn't spared any of the wraths that were dealt to me. He, too, was the subject of kicking and beating whenever mom felt he was out of line. Other than the dog getting the occasional petting, we weren't treated much differently from each other.

There were times that I believed television actually had an influence on the types of punishments she would dole out. As such, my punish-ments began to take on more of an American flair. Mom did not have great command of the English language. I think she may have gotten her ideas from watching old TV sitcoms. For instance, once I was told to wash my mouth out with soap and then eat the soap afterwards. I don't know if she misunderstood what she saw or just added her own touch. I don't think *Dennis the Menace* or *The Beaver*[2] were ever told to eat the soap.

For not liking onions, she would force me to eat a whole onion like an apple. For not eating everything on my plate or eating too slowly, I would be made to sit at the table until it was done or it would be served to me the next morning for breakfast. Liver and lima beans never agreed with me and trying to choke it down the next morning was an experience I wouldn't wish on my worst enemy.

On a different but parallel thought, and in some demented way, I find myself laughing now at my mom's twisted logic; when things were missing, askew, or broken in the house, the blame came directly to me. It was simple and logical; "If I didn't do it and your father didn't do it, and since the dog couldn't do it either; that just leaves you. Therefore, you did it!"

I can't number the amount of times that I was blamed and then beaten for a cracked drinking glass in the sink, missing keys, misplaced earrings, or some other mysterious event. It never mattered whether or not I actually did it, if they didn't do it, who else was there to blame? From an objective point of view, the logic was there; it's deductive reasoning. Sherlock Holmes used it; why couldn't she? She was brilliant! Or was I just a jaded and resigned smartass? It really didn't matter. The consequences were the same either way.

One of the worst beatings I ever took from my father was the one that was the most unwarranted.

One Friday night, we all went out to a Mexican restaurant in Hawthorne, CA. I was on my best behavior and minded all my manners. The waiter took notice of this and complimented my mom and dad on it. As we left, the waiter gave me two helium filled balloons as a reward for saying

---

2 Leave it to Beaver was a sitcom from the late 50's and 60's which still airs today.

Please and *Thank You.* One balloon, supposedly, was for my parents for a job well done and the other was for me.

As we drove home, the one that belonged to my parents had a leak in it. By the time we got home, it had completely deflated. When we got out of the car, my mom lost her mind.

"What the fuck did you to do to my balloon? Why did you pop it? What is your fucking problem!? Are you jealous that I got a balloon too? Do you think you should take all the credit for the way you are!? Get in the fucking house! Take your pants off! I am gonna whip your ass!"

"I didn't do it! It did it by itself; I swear I didn't pop it!"

Any explanation on my part was futile. I went to my room and stripped down to my underwear. Mom's screaming at my dad became louder from the living room.

"You better teach that bastard a lesson! Are you afraid of him? He just laughs at you because you won't touch him! You aren't shit! You chicken shit! You beat his ass until he can't sit!"

She was relentless. She would just lay into him until he couldn't take it anymore. Finally, after an ungodly amount of taunting from her, my father came into my room, furious.

"Why did you do it? Why did you have to pop your mother's balloon?"

On this night, I was scared for my life. I never saw my father so angry. In his hand was a six-inch wide, 1/4-inch thick, three-foot long, crude rubber chest exerciser. On the end of this device were two enclosed plastic handles used for handgrips. My dad had both handles doubled up in one hand.

"Bend over your desk! Each time you scream, you'll get another!"

As I bent over and braced myself, I watched my dad swing way behind his back, and with full force the rubber came down square on my bottom as it made a loud "SMACK!" I screamed like I had never screamed in my life. The pain was unlike anything I had ever felt before.

"That will get you another!"

"Please Daddy! Oh my God, please no Daddy, pleeease no!"

He wound up again and my knees buckled before he made contact, hitting me on my lower back. Again I screamed and begged for mercy.

"That's another!"

The pain was excruciating. I couldn't get up. He picked me up by the back of my neck to stand me up and continued. My legs wobbled and I couldn't get any more words out of my mouth. There wasn't enough air in my lungs to emit any more sounds.

I don't remember how many times he whipped me that night. All I can remember was lying on my side on the floor in the fetal position.

Soon afterwards, Mom walked into the room and told me to get my ass off the floor and into bed. Somehow I managed to crawl up to the bed. I slept on my stomach for the next three days.

Come Monday, I was barely able to sit in the chair of my desk at school. My buttocks and the top part of my rear thighs were black and blue for many, many days.

On a different but congruent thought, and in some demented way, I find myself laughing now at my mom's twisted logic; when things were missing, awry, or broken in the house, the blame came directly to me. It was simple and logical; "If I didn't do it and your father didn't do it, and since the dog couldn't do it either; that just leaves you. Therefore, you did it!"

THE CHRISTMAS GIFT

In 1975, my father was assigned to the 2nd Infantry Division in Wurzburg, Germany. Moving from one country to another was difficult, but it was the military lifestyle. Making friends and keeping them was a constant challenge for military dependents.

Since the word *allowance* was not in my parent's vocabulary, I learned the value of money and understood what it took to earn and appreciate it at an early age. I always found a way to be resourceful and always found a way to earn my own money. For example, while Dad was stationed stateside, I would pick up after the neighbor's dogs for $2.00 a week and mow lawns for $5.00, which included front, back, side, trimming and edging.

Living overseas didn't present such opportunities to make money, but I was diligent and got a job at the base commissary bagging groceries for tips. It was a job I prided myself in because I was one of the youngest on the bagging crew.

I was fast and as skilled as the teen boys. Fifty cents a bag was the average, and a dollar was a big bonus. Coming home with thirty to forty dollars at the end of a shift was excellent. When I got home, I would be allowed to keep the loose change and the paper money went to Mom to put into my imaginary savings account. If there ever was such an account and I could have access to it, I'd be rich today just off the interest.

Due to the overseas move, Mom had to give up her job at *Teledyne Relays* building circuit boards. She too, had to find another way to supplement Dad's meager military income.

She ended up taking a job cleaning stairwells of the four story military housing apartments we lived in. This entailed hand sweeping every landing and every step with a handheld broom. This was then completed by mopping those same steps, also by hand. She had to do four stairwells and when this did not make enough money, she took another job cleaning the elementary school rooms where I went to school.

This work, too, was labor intensive. All the school desks had to be moved to one corner of the room to allow for a thorough sweeping and mopping. The process had to be repeated to clean the area where the desks were moved. When she took on more than she could handle, I was given the option to do one or the other jobs when her schedules overlapped.

While other eleven year old kids were playing outside, I was on my hands and knees cleaning stairwells, mopping floors and hating life. I figured I'd be in for a great Christmas that year for helping my mom out since I was not given an allowance from helping her with these jobs.

When the Christmas season rolled in with the first winter's snowfall, the anticipation of opening gifts on Christmas morning was palpable. This especially rings true when gifts are laid under the Christmas tree three weeks before Christmas day.

In my case, it was a huge 3'x3'x4' tall box that sat next to, and not under, the Christmas tree because it was so big. I couldn't believe how big that box was! What could possibly require such a big box?! When Mom and Dad were in the kitchen, I snuck over to the box and quickly lifted it to see how heavy it was. I could barely lift it!

Oh my God, what could it be? Why was it so heavy? I was flustered with excitement! I'd never received anything so ginormous! My mind was racing! Was it a bike that needed to be put together; maybe a motocross bike or a Go Cart? Maybe it was a bunch of toys all wrapped into one big box! For the next three weeks I fantasized what could possibly be in that big box. It was fun to imagine the possibilities.

I told all of my friends and they were pretty envious, but excited just the same. We all made a game of it that whoever came closest to the right guess would be able to play with it right after me. I think most of my friends wanted to be at my house on Christmas morning instead of at their own! It was cool to be the envy of the block!

Needless to say, I could not sleep on Christmas Eve. The anticipation was unbearable. I probably didn't fall asleep until five in the morning, but I was up by six! The anticipation only grew since it was the tradition to have a big breakfast first and then open gifts afterwards.

When it came time, I was told to open the smaller gifts first. The underwear and socks were quickly opened and tossed to the side as most kids would do.

Now it was time for the unveiling! I looked at Dad and he gave me the nod of approval. I walked over to the box and dragged it away from the tree so as not to break any ornaments while pulling whatever was inside out of the box.

I slowly took off the ribbon and set it to one side. I was compelled to rip the wrapping off like a crazed madman but thought better of it.

When the box was revealed, it was a box that my dad had to get from the moving company, so this had to be special. It was duct taped shut so there was no chance of peeking into it. My dad knew that my curiosity might have gotten the best of me so it was well secured like a mini Fort Knox!

When I opened the top of the box and peered in, there were crumpled newspapers all the way to the top. Whatever was inside, I thought, had to be protected. I mustn't get any scratches on the chrome. I removed the top layer of newspaper only to discover more crumpled newspaper which covered more newspaper. Whatever it was, it was getting smaller with each layer of paper I removed. What could be so heavy and yet so small?

The answers lie three quarters down into the box; cinder blocks! There were four, one in each corner of the box. In the middle, framed by the concrete pillars was something orange. When I reached into the box to pull it out, it was just a deflated basketball and nothing else! Dad didn't even take time to get it inflated for me.

I felt as deflated as the basketball. Even so, I choked back my true emotions. I faked a big smile and even managed a forced laugh with him.

"That's a good one Dad! You got me on that one; pretty funny stuff there, Ha-ha." He thought it was pretty funny too.

I put on my boots, coat and gloves and went downstairs to the basement to get a bicycle pump to fill it up. From there I went to the outdoor basketball court just outside of our apartment complex where Mom and Dad could see me enjoy my new Christmas gift.

The sound of the ball hitting the half foot of snow on the basketball court made for an interesting thud sound when it hit the ground. I could only manage to shoot baskets and then retrieve the ball from the half foot of snow just underneath the basketball hoop. I shot baskets for two hours; shoot, swish, thud, trudge, trudge, trudge. Lather, rinse, repeat.

It was just a matter of time until the other kids came out to play with their new sleds, bikes and other cool stuff. I could see them pointing and laughing at me. It would be the most memorable Christmas in my life; even to this day.

PUBLIC HUMILIATION

It is said that children are resilient. Even so, there is a breaking point. Mine was not the physical abuse; it was the public humiliation that I was put through. If Mom really wanted to break me, she knew that publicly humiliating me was the best way to do it. She wanted complete submission and control over me.

Marbles were a commodity when I was ten-years-old. All the boys would bring their favorite *shooters*, *spirals*, and *granddaddies* to school.

We would totally engross ourselves in a game of *potsie* where the object was to win a pot of marbles that was anted up before the game.

One winter day, I decided to stay a few minutes after school to play a round. I only lived about 200-yards away from the elementary school, so I didn't think it was a big deal. Soon I would find out otherwise.

We could not have been more than ten minutes into the game when I lined up for my shot. I was so focused on getting my shot into the hole that I didn't look up to see the pale, bloodless faces of my buddies staring at a point behind me.

As I bent down on one knee, the next thing I felt was a hard blunt kick that was placed exactly midline of my buttocks. The impact of the kick was so hard that it actually lifted me off the ground sending me face first into the playground sand. Before I could even look around to see what had hit me, another kick was placed right into the back of my spine. The only thing I could think of at the moment was some school bully had decided to target me for soccer practice.

"Get up you son-of-a-bitch! Who the hell said you could stay out to play? Get your fucking ass home right now!"

I was mortified. I looked at my friends briefly and saw the fear in their eyes. They only witnessed a glimpse of things to come. I ran home completely demeaned. I felt an inch tall again. It was the same feeling I remembered from standing out on the porch naked. This was only a harbinger of things to come. On this day I would be introduced to the Military Police baton.

I knew I was in for a beating. Mom had been beating me with a broom handle, but that was getting expensive. The handles would break from the impact with my skull or forearms.

When Mom got home, she told me she had something new for me. She went into the hallway closet and pulled out a three-foot, black billy club. On the end of it was a leather wrist strap. It was at least four inches in diameter at the thickest end and about 22" long and was made of solid oak. It looked like a miniature bat with circular grooves where the handle was. It was what the Military Police would carry as part of their standard issued equipment. Since my dad worked as a supply sergeant, it wasn't uncommon for him to bring home things he had gained from bartering with soldiers from other units. However, I don't believe that he brought this home for the purpose of beating me with it.

She immediately came at me jabbing the stick at my chest and stomach. I backed up until I felt the corner wall of my room. I had nowhere to go and that's when the baton beatings started. The only way I could fend off the blows was to use my hands, wrists, and forearms. When the beating on my forearms surpassed my pain threshold, I would just curl into a ball, protect my head with my hands and take the rest of the beatings with my back, shoulders, and legs. When she got tired, she would kick me a few more times for good measure.

"Wait 'til your father gets home! You are gonna get it! I hope he really kicks your ass!"

Therein lay the real torture. Watching the clock for the next two hours was pure hell. My dad always tried to talk sense into my mom. He never wanted to physically hit me, but she knew exactly what buttons to push to infuriate him. Her ritual tongue-lashing always consisted of demeaning him.

"You are a sorry ass! You are afraid of him! He thinks you aren't shit because you are scared to hit him! What in the hell is wrong with you? Why are you afraid of him, you chicken shit?" was her mantra.

As usual, she was relentless. My father had no choice. She was the dominant figure in the house and what she said went. If not, she would just continue to argue with him until he gave in. She was unshakable.

My father came into the room and closed the door. He told me to sit down and then he explained to me that he never believed in hitting me. His father never physically disciplined him.

As he told me this, I would look into his bloodshot eyes. Mom wore him out. I felt sorry for him. He said he had no choice in the matter. This is what Mom wanted so this is what Mom would get. I knew he meant it.

In a *let's get this over with* tone of voice, he would tell me to hold on to the desk and try not to buckle. He didn't want to hit me anywhere else that wasn't necessary. Ten whips was the standard. If he didn't do a good job, the arguing would continue. It always took at least a couple of days before I could sit normally again.

One of the most profound moments I recall with Dad was when he beat the bed instead of me. He told me to yell when he struck the bed so Mom would think it was me. It was this that convinced me that Dad really never wanted to hit me. Mom's power on him was mindboggling.

3

Adolescent Years (1979-1982)

My ADOLESCENT YEARS were the worst part of my life. From the age of twelve to seventeen the abuse and hatred intensified from my mother. It seems the older I got, the more she hated me. I started to keep a journal from this point. By keeping a journal I was able to write down all my thoughts and just shelve them away and not have to think about anything that depressed me. It was my vent; my outlet.

I wrote daily and documented in it every time she decided I would be used as her punching bag. I didn't hide the journal and I knew she was reading it when I was at school. All it did was infuriate her at the truths that I was writing. I have no idea why she didn't destroy these danger-ously incriminating journals.

To this day, I have all my journals from those years and I am amazed at all the things I went through during my teen years. I wouldn't want to go back to that time period for all the money in the world.

Mom's abuse towards me now progressed from open-handed slaps to my head to closed fist punches to my face. She would actually ball her fists and punch me in the face like a boxer. Kicking now became stomping. Like a horse, she would try to trample me into the ground. Any exposed part of my body was fair game. If it wasn't covered, it was a target.

Another new punishment was to tell me how ugly or inadequate I was. She would pull me by my hair and drag me across the floor to the bathroom. I was forced to look in the mirror at the lumps and welts on my face while she insulted me.

"How can anyone love you? Look at your ugly ass face! You are ugly! How can you even stand to look at yourself? Nobody loves you and nobody will. No wonder your mother got rid of you!"

Her favorite thing to tell me was that I would amount to nothing. She said as soon as I turned eighteen, she didn't want to have anything to do with me nor was I ever to return to the house.

Then I'd tell her that would never happen and she had no worries about me ever coming back. Of course this remark would only anger her more and that automatically commenced with more beatings.

I don't know what made her think that I would ever want to come back to that house.

Everyday I'd fantasize about the day I turned eighteen. It didn't matter if I had nowhere to go or even if I had no money to get there. Living as a transient would have been the ultimate million-dollar dream for me. Freedom is priceless.

The older I got, the more stoic I became. I wouldn't flinch or cry when she punched me in the face. I would just stand there and give her a blank stare and this angered her even more. Because of this, Mom added a new weapon to her arsenal.

The ultimate degradation now came in the form of spitting. After a barrage of verbal insults, she would emphasize her point by spitting in my face. I felt lower than low. If there was any connection that was left of a son to his mother, it was this action that finally disconnected me from any bonds I had with her.

Even though I accepted the physical and mental abuse, I felt that no mother, biological or adopted, would ever spit on her child. This was the lowest point in my life. My true hatred for her only intensified. What little respect I had left for her as a mother was now gone. I swore to myself that one day, somehow, I would exact my revenge.

MY FIRST CRUSH GETS CRUSHED

Having a girlfriend during my teen years made life tolerable. In 1979, I entered the 9th grade. We had just left Germany and my dad retired from the military. We moved to a small town in southern California called Gardena. It was a highly populated town of 1st – 3rd generation Japanese. Being raised by a Japanese mother and living in Japan, it was a culture I identified with. I was happy to move there. However, I soon found out that even though I identified with the culture, it did not identify with me.

I wasn't as accepted as I wanted to be. I didn't look Japanese nor did I have a Japanese last name. Given this and the fact that I was an *outsider* made it tough to adapt to my new school environment.

In my English class, however, there was a cute Japanese girl by the name of *Wendy*. She sat in front of me and made me forget that I was the class reject. She was curious about me and she'd turn around every once in a while and talk to me. She was nice and she'd let me walk her to her next class. Eventually, we became an item and she turned out to be my first *crush*.

It was also during this time that the abuse from my mom became more and more intense.

Wendy provided me an escape. She was my grounding and my validation. She made me feel wanted and important. She gave me something to look forward to everyday. When mom would beat me, afterwards I would lose myself in writing long letters to Wendy or re-reading the ones she had sent me in return. I took all her letters and encased each one in a clear plastic sheet protector that I'd put into a three ring binder.

In time, the binder could barely hold all of her letters. The beatings didn't seem to matter anymore. I had someone who cared and loved me. It was an extraordinary feeling. I felt alive!

When Mom discovered I had a girlfriend from all the letters I kept, she was furious! She said I was too young and I shouldn't be involved with girls at all. Even though she had never met Wendy, I could tell that she hated her. I didn't understand it. She told me to stay away from her but that only made me want to see her more.

Back in those days, the newspaper was delivered by young kids on bicycles. I was one of them. The work wasn't easy but it gave me some freedom to get out of the house and make some money (although I saw very little of it).

One paper route was grueling enough, but when another route became available that had Wendy's street address on it, I jumped on it! What should have taken an hour and a half to deliver those papers, would actually take three hours, especially, since I would always stop at her house to see her.

When Mom found out I was riding my bike to her house after school, she said I was obsessed and too young to have one steady girlfriend.

In my 10th grade year, those who received a 3.5 GPA were awarded a pair of Dodger tickets. With my passion for baseball and having already been to several professional baseball games, I was excited to attend. Dad was a huge Dodger fan and it would be exciting to go to the game and enjoy some bonding time with him. However, on this day, Mom decided it was time for me to break things up between Wendy and me.

For no reason at all, Mom dialed Wendy's number and got her on the phone. She told her that I had something to tell her, called me over, handed me the phone, and told me to break up with her. I was dumbfounded and didn't know what to say. I stumbled for words, still reeling on what was happening.

The only thing that I could say was "my mom said I have to break up with you."

With that, Mom grabbed the phone and told her to stay away from me and slammed the phone down.

I was mortified, devastated, and humiliated yet again. I was in an absolute state of shock. I went to my room, shut the door and couldn't stop crying. This was worse than the cursing or beatings. She won. She finally got to the core of my soul and beat me down completely. I couldn't take it. I felt this was the bottom of the bottoms. I never felt lower than what I was feeling at that point. I felt like I had nothing left in me; less than zero.

Then night Dad came into the room and asked me if I was ready to go.

"No Dad. You and Mom can go. I got a lot of homework."

After they left, I went into the bathroom medicine cabinet and found a bottle of aspirin. There wasn't anything stronger. I took a mouthful of water and emptied the bottle of aspirin into my mouth. The bottle was about three quarters full. That should put me out of my misery. Since aspirin was a pain killer, this should be painless, I thought. I laid down and was just happy that this life was soon going to be over. No more senseless beatings or cursing. Anyplace had to better than this, even if it were Hell.

When I woke up, I felt nauseous. I wasn't sure how long I slept, but it was dark outside and Mom and Dad were still not home. When I tried to get up to go to the bathroom, I was dizzy and fell to the ground. I was really weak.

When I crawled to the toilet, I tried to throw up but couldn't get anything to come up. I crawled back to bed. I didn't want Mom to find me sick on the bathroom floor. She'd be mad and would be beat me.

When I got back into bed, I realized things weren't going as planned. It was supposed to be painless and easy; neither of which this turned out to be. I felt like I was slipping in and out of consciousness.

When Mom and Dad came home, Mom came into my room to check on me. She was surprised to see me lying on top of my bedcovers and asked me what the hell was wrong with me.

I told her I didn't feel good and thought I was coming down with something.

She told me to *sleep it off*.

For the next two days my stomach was killing me and I couldn't eat anything. I was in pretty bad shape. To this day, they are clueless as to what I tried to do.

As far as Wendy was concerned, I resigned myself to letting her go. Mom would only make my life worse if I attempted to call or see her. It was a very dark period in my life during that time.

We only stayed in Gardena for one year.

My parents found a home in Carson which was a few cities away and I was transplanted, yet again, to another school. I was devastated. I wouldn't see Wendy again and I felt as if my lifeblood was going to drain with every day that I didn't get to see her.

WORK AND NOTHING TO SHOW FOR IT

In the summer of 1980, Mom decided she wanted to put a pool into our backyard. She figured the best way to save money was to dig the hole ourselves. The *ourselves*, of course, turned out to be me. This is how I spent the summer of 1980.

For two months, I dug a hole; a very big hole. There was no budget for a back hoe or other heavy equipment. I was given a shovel and I was sarcastically happy because it wasn't a hand gardening shovel. It was a real two-handed shovel! Lucky me!

At the end of two months and buckets of sweat and manual labor, the hole was huge. One day she came out the backyard and made an executive decision. She decided that the pool was not a good idea after all. So for the remaining part of that summer, guess what I had to do? Yup, fill in the hole I just dug. Inwardly, I laughed hysterically. Why was my fate becoming one big, sick joke?

The following summer, prior to my senior high school year, the neighbor across the street offered me a job at *Manhattan Beach Unified School District* where he was the Superintendent of the Maintenance Department. I was hired on as an apprentice and would assist with whatever the maintenance crew needed me to do. It was a job that no one else wanted to do, but it was a great way for me to get out of the house and make some money again. Nine dollars an hour for a seventeen year old was a lot of money back then when minimum wage was just over three dollars per hour.

I learned how to replace broken tiles, fix locks, paint, landscape, and tar roofs. I found myself tarring roofs more than anything else since

that was the least favorite thing for anyone else to do. It was a grueling job and the rooftops would get in excess of 110-120 degrees in
the mid-afternoons. My work boots would literally melt as I'd slop the
tar down with an old mop. In the end, however, I enjoyed what I did. I
wasn't at home getting a beat down or digging and filling in holes for
nothing.

Unfortunately, my only method of getting to work was to rely on Mom
for a ride. It was a little bit of a way from Carson to Manhattan Beach. She
would tally up how much the gas was and remind me daily of how much
time, effort and gas she was using taking me back and forth to work. I
promised to pay her back when I got my check. She told me to sign the
check over to her and she would deduct what I owed her and put the rest
into her account for safekeeping. It was likely the same mysterious account where all the other money I earned ended up.

It was just a matter of time before she got tired of taking me to work.
I asked if we could use the money I was making to buy a moped and she
agreed. A low-end model would cost around $900.

After a month, I calculated that I had saved enough to pay for it.

When I got it, there was a sense of freedom that I cannot describe. It
was only 50cc and got up to 45mph going downhill, but it was great! I felt
I could go to the end of the world on that little moped.

At the end of that summer, my job at the school district was complete. I wasn't sure how much money I made, but I knew it was at least
three thousand dollars. That was more money than I had ever made in my
lifetime. When I asked my mom how much I had, she replied, "Nothing.
You still owe me money!" I wasn't a math genius, but my calculations
could not have been that far off. At nine dollars and hour, forty hours
a week, four weeks per month; I should have grossed about $4,320.00.
Was I in the upper 1% of the tax bracket? How did I owe more than what
I made? The moped couldn't have been more than $1100.00 with tax and
registration.

I asked her how much I owed her and why. Her simple response was,
"gas, food, housing, clothes, healthcare..." I had failed to figure in that

living at home with my parents now became a home care facility. I wasn't about to argue with her. I just chalked up another one in the back of my mind and simply responded with 'Oh, okay'.

BLIND EYES

When society turns a blind eye to an abused child, the feeling of hopelessness is magnified a thousand fold. Helplessness is overwhelming when neighbors and law enforcement look away at a child's moment of shear desperation. I experienced this firsthand.

It was a Saturday summer morning and I was recovering from a long week of tarring roofs at my work. After punching me in the face several times in the backyard and dropping me to my knees I threatened mom with calling the police. I don't remember why she punched me but actually it didn't matter. She never needed a good reason to beat me.

"What the fuck do you think the police are going to do? They can't do shit! You wanna call the police? Go right the fuck ahead! Better yet, I'll call them for you!"

I don't know what she said on the phone, but the Sheriff Deputies showed up. I was still on my knees in the backyard. I felt relieved when they showed up. Once and for all I was going to prove that this type of beating was against the law. When I was younger I believed the way I was punished was normal. I thought that other kids were punished the same way I was. But after hearing them complain about getting grounded or privileges taken away, I now began to believe otherwise. She wasn't going to get away with it anymore!

"Okay, so here they are. Now what are you going to do?"

As the officers watched and before I could respond, she swung back and punched me in the face again.

She looked back at the officers and then back to me.

"You see! They aren't going to do shit to me!"

I reeled back from the punch and waited for the Sheriff Deputies to arrest her. But they didn't. They just looked at me pathetically and shook their heads. They didn't do anything! They just stood there! I was floored. This couldn't be happening! It was unbelievable!

"Is there anything else we can do here, ma'am?" the deputy asked.

She told them that it was all under control and would call them again if I ever got out of hand. I'm sure she told them that I was under the influence of drugs or some other lie. There couldn't be any other explanation. I have a difficult time believing that officers of the law would just walk away from a scene like that.

Afterwards, I got up and headed for my best friend Jaime Sanchez's house. We lived in a cul-de-sac and the neighbors came out to see what the police were doing in the neighborhood. My face was red and swollen from the beating. I felt like a rejected Citadel plebe walking down the gauntlet of shame. Looking down at the sidewalk, in my peripheral vision, I could see the neighbors staring then turning away as I got closer to their houses. I became that naked five-year-old left out the porch again.

Jaime's father was home when I knocked on the door. He took one look at me and was horrified. He asked me what had happened and I told him. He couldn't believe what I was telling him could actually happen at the hands of a mother, but he knew it was the truth. Jaime witnessed the abuse on many occasions when he came to visit. It was one of Mom's favorite times to humiliate me. Mr. Sanchez said Jaime had told him about it but he couldn't bring himself to believe it. He believed it now. He offered his home as a sanctuary and told me to stay as long as I needed to.

I stayed for a couple of days until things calmed down. Mom, through neighbors, found out where I was staying. I was only a block away so it was just a matter of time before she came knocking at the door.

Mr. Sanchez answered and I knew he was going to get an earful. Mom would attempt to convince him that I was hell spawned and it would be best for me to return home where I could be "handled." I thought Mr. Sanchez would give in, but he held his ground and told her to leave. I felt as though God had given me a guardian angel. Mom threatened him with a lawsuit and reminded him of what was and wasn't his business. He politely told her where she could go and demanded she get off his property.

When she finally left, I couldn't find the words to express my gratitude to Jamie's dad. He was my savior and all I could muster was, "Thank you, Mr. Sanchez."

I couldn't impose on Mr. Sanchez for too long. I needed clothes, school supplies, and I felt badly that I couldn't contribute to groceries. I always thanked him and he would just give me a warm smile and an assuring hand on the shoulder.

Eventually, however, I returned home.

At first things were quiet, but it was like a slow simmering cauldron waiting to boil over. Mom just gave me the '*I knew you would come back*' look.

It was just another typical day after school. I came home immediately from school, did my chores, and then immersed myself in my homework. That was my getaway and my excuse to avoid any confrontations with Mom.

An hour had passed since I returned home from school, and the house was really quiet. I guessed Mom was out in the yard or visiting with the neighbor.

There was no warning, no sound, and no clue for what happened next.

The next thing I can remember was a sharp painful blow to the right side of my head. It was so hard that I fell sideways out of my chair. A barrage of kicks immediately followed to my back and then more punches to my head. I covered up and waited until she tired.

When she was done I asked her *what was that for?*

"You figure it out!" She said, "When you do, come tell me!"

I ended up confessing to a whole bunch of things that I thought may have warranted this beating; *I didn't clean up the dog poop, didn't empty the trash can, didn't wash the dishes?*

The reasons I gave her weren't the ones she was looking for. The more reasons I thought of as to why I was getting beat, only led to more punches to my head.

In all the other situations where my mom beat me, she had a *reason*. However, there was no logic or rationale for this. I concluded that it was a delayed reaction to the embarrassment she felt at Mr. Sanchez's house.

4

The Last Beating

AN OVERABUNDANCE OF teenage testosterone led to weight lifting, which became my obsession. I started to put on muscle and weight and competed that year in our high school bodybuilding contest. Along with that testosterone, *Playboy Magazines* found their way between my mattresses (well, okay, I put them there). And like any curious mother (mine more than others it seemed), somehow, they found their way into her hands.

The old adage of "Hell hath no fury like a women scorned" was no longer true to me. Hell was not familiar with my mom...yet.

"You mother-fucking sex maniac! Where the fuck did you get these? You will never bring shit like this into my house again!"

She left my bedroom for a brief minute. My mind was whirling. I had never seen her so infuriated. This was the worst. My brain couldn't think fast enough. I could only brace myself for what was about to come. When it did, I wasn't prepared for it.

She came back with a baseball bat!

She came at me swinging hard and fast. My normal reaction would have been to double up and protect my head. This time I reacted differently. Now I was bigger and stronger and I quickly turned my body so I was facing the bat squarely as it came down. I held up both hands and caught the bat at the end and the middle. She wouldn't let go.

With all my weight, I spun her around as we both held onto the bat and with a quick jerk forward then back, she stumbled backwards onto the bed.

She was dumbfounded. Her eyes were wide with disbelief and she didn't move. I stood over her with my finger pointing inches away from her face.

"Never, will you never ever, fucking touch me again! Do you understand? Never!" I yelled.

Holding the bat, I walked out of the house and into the garage. I started up my moped and sped off.

As I exited the driveway, she came out of the house cursing profanities.

In response, I held my left fist high in the air with my middle finger proudly at full attention. At the top of my lungs I yelled *fuck you!*

At that moment I felt complete freedom. It was deliverance pure and simple. There was no feeling like it in the world. For all those years of emotional and physical abuse, it all came down to this one last event. It was absolute rapture. I was finally free and nobody would ever hurt me again the way she hurt me.

I drove to the beach. That was my haven.

In all the times I ran away, it was there I found my tranquility, serenity, peace and solace. Everything seemed so pure and unblemished there. Nothing and nobody could touch me here. Once and for all I felt undiminished peace. I knew I wasn't going back. The child was gone and in his place was a young man determined to become someone. I would prove her wrong.

In the meantime, Mr. Sanchez let me stay at his home.

COMMUNITY COLLEGE MOLESTATION

Prior to graduating from high school, I started to take night classes at the local community college. Chemistry and Geometry were two courses that I needed to graduate and taking them earlier in the year would give me a reprieve prior to graduating.

I had to ride my bike from home to the college. Although it was only 10 miles away, it was physically and mentally taxing after being in school all day to take two additional classes at night. Trying to understand the periodic tables and the principles of neutrons, protons, and electrons had me reeling. I struggled with the course.

One night at the end of class, my Chemistry instructor stopped me and asked me how I was coming along. My exams were far from stellar and he knew I was struggling.

Mr. McGowan (not his real name) was an older and short man, perhaps around 60 or so. He had gray hair around the temples and bald on top. I remember his uneven and stained teeth. He wasn't the most aesthetically pleasing person to look at, but that's not why I was there. I just needed to pass this course to graduate from high school and didn't care what my instructor looked like.

He asked me if I needed some after class help and I gladly accepted. He said he had time right now and had an instructor's office that we could go to. He said it would prevent other students from interrupting us since no one was allowed in the instructor's office.

When we got there, the door was locked and there were blinds on the glass door window. We went inside and he closed and locked the door behind him.

He took out his grading book to see where I stood on the grading curve then asked me why I was taking the course. I explained that it was a requirement to graduate from high school.

"So you really need this course don't you? As it stands now, you are barely at a D minus. What will you do to pass this course?"

"Whatever it takes," I quickly responded.

I wanted to convey my willingness to study extra hard with whatever additional course or supplemental materials or help that he could give me.

He looked straight into my eyes and raised an eyebrow, "Really?"

There wasn't another chair in the room so he told me to sit on his desk and relax. He walked over to me and started rubbing my neck and shoulders. He said I looked stressed and thought I could use a massage. He grabbed my thigh and asked me if I worked out.

When he saw my uncomfortable reaction, he stopped.

"Let's get you some study aids. They will be helpful and I assure you that you will pass the course if you follow my instructions. Sound good to you?"

I refocused on passing the course and graduation and affirmed his plan. He said that the materials were at a colleague's place just down the street and we could drive there in two minutes. I told him I'd follow him on my bike, but he insisted that I ride with him and he'd bring me back as soon as we got what he needed.

I'm not sure what happened to my mind at this point or even at the point when he put his hands on my leg. It was as if my mind took me out of my own body and I was able to watch this whole scenario unfold in front of my eyes. It was surreal. It was as if I was being safely disconnected from the physical world around me.

We drove into a trailer park and up to a single wide trailer. He told me to come in and have a seat.

I entered, and sat down on an old beat up sofa chair and looked around. There was a myriad of books on shelves, an old TV, a fish tank with a couple of fish in it and an old lamp nearby. It was not a neat place nor was it in disarray; it just didn't seem to be a place that a college professor would live in, or be a place one professor would share with another for instructional purposes.

From the kitchen, Mr. McGowan asked me if I wanted a drink. Thinking he was offering me a soda or some water, I politely declined even though my mouth was dry.

When I answered, I looked over my shoulder and saw him take a drink of something in a short glass. I am not sure what it was, but imagine it to be something strong to give him the courage to do what he was going to do next.

He came over to where I was sitting and stood directly in front of me. "If you want to pass the course, you know what to do," he said as he started unzipping his fly.

In my mind, I knew I was bigger and stronger than he was. I could easily overpower him and even kill him if I had to. What my body wanted to do and what my mind wanted to do, however, were two separate things.

I couldn't get my brain to synch up with my body. Rather than standing up and shoving him through a wall or two, I simply looked up at him and said, "I don't plan on doing that."

He looked at me disgustingly and said, "Okay, that's your choice."

He drove me back to where my bike was and nothing was said. I never returned to that class again. I expected to get an incomplete or a fail for the course, but it turned out that he gave me a C.

I'm assuming he feared that I'd turn him in. Turns out, it wouldn't be the last time I'd see him. By pure chance, I would run into him again a few years later.

From this experience and to this day, I subconsciously and physically flinch whenever a man touches my shoulder. It's an auto response that I can't help.

GRADUATION SPEECH AND THE DISAPPOINTED LOOKS

I graduated at the top of my class and was awarded the category of Class Ephebian[3]. I was also asked to give the graduation speech.

In my speech, I used the analogy of climbing a mountain and reaching the top only to see more mountains in the distance that had to be conquered. *This pinnacle was only one of many to overcome.* I added *that if it weren't for our parents, that this climb would not have been possible.* I thought that Mom and Dad would be proud of me for putting that into the speech.

---

3 The Ephebian Society is a civic betterment and service organization whose membership is composed of citizens who are graduated from the Los Angeles area high schools and selected for membership in the society by the faculties and senior classes of their high schools. They are selected on the basis of outstanding character, leadership, demonstrated service, and high scholastic achievement, which is defined by the Society as a 3.3 cumulative grade point average (4.0 max scale).

When I said this part of the speech, I paused and looked into the crowd as I received a round of applause.

I saw Mom and Dad and they weren't even smiling or clapping. They looked disappointed.

When the speech was over, I watched as parents hugged their kids and gave congratulatory high fives, kisses, cards and gifts. I, on the other hand, got nothing except *so it looks like you'll be off to the Army.*

That was it; no hug, high five, or even a *good luck.*

While my classmates went off with their parents and relatives to graduation dinners and parties, I went to Jaime's house and started to pack what little I could take to *Army Basic Training.*

The following week, my recruiter picked me up early in the morning. Again there was no send off, good luck, or pat on the back from my parents and I didn't expect it. It was par for the course.

5

Joining the Military (1982)

As MUCH I dreamt of going to Stanford University, there were never any plans by my parents to send me to a private college. As far back as I could remember it was always grilled into me that I would be attending *West Point Military Academy.* Since Dad was an Army veteran, it guaranteed me a Presidential nomination to the academy. It was something that my dad badly wanted for me. I think it was that point alone that deterred me from completing that dream with him. It was *his* dream and not mine.

In the first semester of my senior high school year, I resigned myself that I wouldn't be going to college or even *West Point* for that matter. Actually, the only thing that mattered to me was to get out of the house as soon as I possibly could upon graduation.

Since I was only seventeen years old, my enlistment was contingent upon parental consent. When the recruiter came over with the enlistment contract, there wasn't any hesitation on the part of my parents to sign on the dotted line. If fact, it almost seemed to be a huge relief for them when they did.

Soon after signing, I took my ASVAB test, scored high and qualified for many different fields. I chose to go into communications since it came with a $25,200.00 *Army College Fund* incentive.

On July 6th of 1982, right after graduating from high school, I found myself running from an old green military bus with other recruits, while drill sergeants yelled at us from every direction.

I was somewhere in Alabama and the humid heat was punishing.

In a matter of minutes, we were all drenched in sweat from doing push-ups. I felt as if we were all trying to push the earth away from the sun.

While standing in formation, many of the trainees fell where they stood, a result of locking their knees, combined with the humidity.

It didn't seem to matter that the drill sergeants kept telling us that locking our knees would restrict blood to the brain. Most of the guys were so scared they couldn't process the information spewing out of the drill sergeants' mouth.

For most, basic training was the toughest thing that my cohorts had ever encountered. They weren't used to yelling and taking orders on a dime. I felt bad for the guys that cried at night in their bunks. I'd find myself getting out of my rack and trying to get their spirits up. I kept telling them that it was part of the game and we'd all make it through if we just stuck together as a team.

Obviously, I had no problems adapting to this *hostile* environment. All I had to do was what I was told to do, excel in all the things I had to learn, follow orders, and be compliant. It was what I'd been doing for the last 17 years. The only difference was, here in Basic Training, I was validated every time I excelled in a task.

What I endured prior to basic training was ten times worse than what basic training had to offer. Hell, these drill sergeants weren't even allowed to hit us or use profanity! To top it off, I got paid and was allowed to actually keep my money and do whatever I wanted to do with it. What a great place to be!

The emotional *hell* that these guys had to face for eight weeks didn't come close to what I had already been experiencing at home. The guys in my platoon couldn't figure out how I was able to keep such a positive attitude.

I knew what they couldn't guess, it was the same attitude that had kept me progressing through my entire life; *I've already been to hell and back. It can't get worse.*

Mentally, basic training was a cakewalk for me. No doubt there were some extreme physical challenges, but I still ended up graduating in the top three of my class. I was proud of myself; while I did have to dig fox holes and defensive battle positions, I wasn't the ditch digger my mom said I would become and I did amount to something.

As the battalion officer prepared to announce the graduating class and top soldiers, I looked out into the stands. Family members of my cohorts were beaming with smiles and tears of pride. What a great moment it must have been for them to be honored by their families who, for many, traveled hundreds of miles.

My fellow soldiers, while trained to maintain their bearing at all times (smiling was not allowed), couldn't keep smiles off their faces. I envied them. The feeling of walking tall and proud in front of their family was one that I would never come to know. It would be one of many of my life's accomplishments where there would be no parental validation.

Although being in the military was not difficult for me, being away from home was hard. Despite being raised in an abusive family, and as ironic as it may seem, I missed my mom and dad. One would think that through everything I had been put through, I would have cut ties at this point, but such was not the case. They were still my parents. What could they do to hurt me at this point in my life? I would soon find out.

My first Christmas in the military was spent on a small military base just outside of Wurzburg, Germany. It was the same place where I grew up in my teen years. I only made $752.00 per month, but I would have gladly spent that money to go home to my parents and enjoy a home cooked meal.

I sent a letter in November of that year and told them I was coming home for Christmas. I assumed they missed me too and would be happy to have me home.

I was wrong.

When I got a return letter from my dad, I couldn't wait to see their excited response. I knew my mom would be excited about making all my favorite food and having her son home for Christmas to be a reunited family again. After all, the previous Christmases were not exactly family-oriented since I had left home to live with a friend and his family.

When I opened the letter and read what my dad wrote, I sat where I stood and fell into instant depression.

Dear Son,

We don't think it's a good idea for you to come for Christmas. Save your money and when your tour in Germany is completed, we will see you then.....

And that is all I can remember from that letter.

My buddy Dave, who had gone through Basic Training with me, and I spent Christmas Eve at the *Enlisted Men's Club* playing Galaga (an *old school* arcade game) and getting drunk.

I remembered looking outside the window that night to a semi-deserted military base and watching the snow come down. I felt alone and disconnected. It was one of the most depressing holiday seasons that I can remember.

Soon after Christmas, I was reassigned to a small outpost outside of Nuremberg. It was an easy assignment. On a mountaintop, in the middle of what felt like the middle of nowhere, my job was to maintain multi-channel equipment to ensure 24-hour communication for the *32ndAir Defense Command.* It was a live mission in case East Germany decided to invade West Germany.

It was a pretty stress-free assignment. We worked 24-hour shifts with one day off, and would vary the shifts so we'd have 2 days off every once in a while.

Once we were off shift, we were allowed to leave the site and go down the mountain to a small town where we'd drink ourselves into a stupor. It seemed to be the military lifestyle overseas.

We were all homesick and talked about what we would do once we got out. There was camaraderie among those of us in the military (this is difficult to explain to a civilian).

We are a band of brothers, and in battle we would not hesitate to take a bullet for one of our own or put our life in harm's way to protect the other. It comes from basic training where we were taught that we were only as strong as the weakest link. With this, we'd help others get across low crawl courses, breaches, forced 12-mile road marches, or any obstacle that was in our way.

And although we could protect each other on the field, there was one thing we could not protect each other from: life circumstances.

It was on rare occasions that an officer and 1st Sergeant would come up to our site unannounced. When they did, it was a mad scramble to get things in order and to present ourselves in the best light possible. However on this day, as the Captain and Top[4] pulled up with his driver in his Humvee and entered our gate, there was a very different look about him. Our Cap[5] was usually very charismatic and smiled in most situations. Today he didn't smile.

Our site Chief walked up to him and saluted and stood at attention as we watched from our day room windows. The captain put our supervisor at ease and then looked down at the ground while he was explaining something that appeared to bother the captain.

We watched the reaction of our site Chief as he hung his head down and motioned for our team leader to come out. The team leader went out and immediately did an about face and returned to the day room.

"Pvt. Markham, the Captain and site Chief need to speak with you."

Pvt. Markham was one of the FNG's[6]. He was only eighteen-years-old and had a baby face that we always teased him about. We had just initi-

---

4 'Top' is a slang term used for 1st Sergeants; top ranking non-commissioned officer.
5 Cap' is short for Captain.
6 A military term of endearment for a new recruit or soldier.

ated him into the platoon the week prior in the small burg at the base of the mountain. German beer and Greek Ouzo did not mix and Pvt. Markham would be the first to tell you so.

We kept watching to see what his reaction would be to whatever the Captain had come to tell him. What kind of trouble did Markham get himself into to warrant a visit from the Captain and Top? It had to be bad.

Whatever it was that the Captain had said to Markham made Markham drop to his knees and start bawling. Top, the Cap, and our site Chief all knelt down in a desperate attempt to console him, but to no avail.

The Section Chief double-timed it back to the day room and told us to get Markham's belongings packed ASAP. His father had died from a multiple coronary and Markham was on his way back to the world.

We packed all his uniforms into his duffle bag and personal belongings into his civilian suitcase. When Markham was brought back to his bunk, he was in a state of shock and couldn't function. We had to dress him in his class-A uniform since he couldn't fly on a civilian aircraft in his BDU's[7].

After him and "the brass" left, we sat in the day room and talked about how we would never want to be in that position. We felt worlds away from our loved ones back in the *States*. This incident only made it feel that much further away.

Two weeks later, Top and the Cap were at our gates again. We all cringed in disbelief. Who was it now?

The same scenario played out before our very eyes. This time, the Section Chief called *me* and told me to see the Captain. I was floored. I couldn't move. I knew what was about to be told to me was not going to be good news.

I double timed over to the Captain and saluted him and he saluted me back. "Stand at ease, PFC[8] Guevara. I have some bad news."

---

7 Battle Dress Uniform
8 Private First Class

He paused for a moment and took a breath. "Your mom had a stroke. You need to call your father ASAP and get your gear together."

My heart and mind were going a million miles an hour as I called my dad. When he picked up the phone, I barely recognized his voice. He normally had a very tough and deep voice, but now he sounded very weak and resigned.

"Dad, what happened?!"

"Your momma had a headache last night, so I helped her to bed early. She's been having these headaches for several days and the doctor prescribed Darvocet. When I woke up to leave for work, I thought she was still sleeping and I didn't want to wake her up. When I got back from work, she was still in bed and wouldn't wake up. I didn't know what to do! I thought she was dead!"

He was hysterical at this point and I asked him where she was.

"She's at UCLA Medical Center. She had a stroke and they are operating on her brain right now to relieve the pressure."

He started to sob and cry. It was the first time I had ever heard him cry. It was unreal and something I thought I'd never experience. I always knew him as a rough, tough, stoic brick wall, but not that day.

I held steady as best I could and told him that everything was going to be okay. I was on my way and would be there soon. I had to remain strong for him at this point. One of us had to be the pillar of support and I took on that role.

I held steady as best I could and told him that everything was going to be okay. I was on my way and would be there soon. I had to remain strong for him at this point. One of us had to be the pillar of support and I took on that role.

When I arrived at LAX, Dad was there as I got off the plane. He looked tired, sad, and his eyes were bloodshot. He still managed to smile and gave me a look of approval. He also hugged me. It was a real hug and not just an obligatory quick pat on the back type of hug. He actually hugged me tight like a father would hug his son. It felt really good.

"The good news is that your momma is in ICU. She made it through surgery. She had a double aneurysm in her brain and the pressure was relieved. The bad news is she is in a coma and the doctors are not making any promises."

His voice got lower in an apologetic tone, "I shouldn't have let her go to sleep. I should have taken her to the hospital. If I had, she would be okay."

"Dad, you didn't know. It's not your fault. Mom is going to be okay."

On the ride home, he explained to me that Mom had taken on a job at a local hotel cleaning rooms. She had been complaining of headaches for a while and they only got worse. The doctors thought it was just a reaction from the cleaning chemicals and prescribed her some pain killers.

After the surgery, the prognosis was not good since there was brain damage from the intracranial pressure. If she came out of the coma, chances were, due to the side of the brain that was affected; she was going to be quadriplegic.

As we arrived at the hospital, he warned me that Mom didn't look the same. He reminded me that she just had a brain operation and to prepare myself to see her. When I walked into the room, I wasn't prepared to see what I did. Mom's head was completely shaven and there were tubes coming out of her from everywhere. I walked to her bedside slowly trying to take in everything and process it all. It was overwhelming and at that point I completely lost it.

I grabbed her hand very gently, "Mom? It's me, Tony. Can you hear me?"

At that very moment, one of her eyes opened and she said through her oxygen mask "Tony? What the hell are you doing here?" I laughed and cried at the same time. She came out of her coma! As she looked around, she tried to get up.

"Mom, you had a stroke. You're in the hospital. Don't move. You're gonna be okay!"

Dad ran over and was beside himself in happiness and was trying to calm and comfort her.

"Vieja[9], you have to stay in bed. You just had an operation. You are going to be fine!" With that, Mom closed her eyes and fell asleep.

A NEW RELATIONSHIP WITH DAD

As the days passed, Mom's prognosis got better and better. We would sit at her bedside for hours and watch TV and when she did wake up, we'd feed her and talk with her. She had a hard time communicating and couldn't form full sentences. Oftentimes she would just start crying from the frustration with the inability to communicate the way she wanted to.

In just three short weeks, Mom was being transferred to an in-house rehabilitative therapy and care center in Downey. She would have to learn how to walk and talk again. The initial prognosis of being quadriplegic was downgraded to paraplegic. In time, that too, would be downgraded to the use of a walker and later to a heavy left side gait.

I think it was just her stubborn will that would not allow her to be anything less than where she was prior to the stroke.

While Mom stayed at the rehab center, Dad returned to work and I was assigned to the very same Recruiting Battalion in Los Angeles that he was assigned to a few years prior. It was ironic I ended up being an Army Recruiter at the same high school in Gardena that my dad recruited out of just a decade and a half prior. In fact, the bigger irony is that I almost served in every outfit in the Army that he had served in.

During my tenure there Dad and I bonded for the first time. We talked a lot about his military career and compared the *new Army* with the *old Army*. We agreed that although there were differences, the same knuckleheads that were spewing orders back then could still be found in today's Army. He talked to me about Vietnam and how hard his tours were over there. He had seen things that he'd never want anyone else to see.

---

9 Endearing term in Spanish for *wife*.

He said it had changed him and although I had not yet seen battle, I felt I could somewhat relate to what he was saying.

Dad found a bar near the hospital. We'd head over there to relax, tip back a few beers and watch the ballgames on the tube. I felt as though we were making up for lost time. He respected me and I could tell he was proud of me and my military career. He'd brag to the others in the bar that I was his son. This was the first time I had ever heard him say he was proud of me for any of my accomplishments. This was a milestone in our relationship. The bonding was awesome, but short-lived.

Mom's recovery was swift. Within a few months, she returned home. She could get around in a walker and cane but still needed constant care and attention. Her temper, however, seemed to be worse than I could ever remember. She would lash out and curse if she couldn't get her way. She would curse at my dad in public and completely humiliate him. The breaking point for me was when she raised her cane and tried to hit me with it.

I had to get out of there ASAP so I moved to a small room in the back of my aunt's house that she rented out to me in downtown Los Angeles.

MR. MCGOWAN REVISITED

On one particular day, I had to give a presentation at the high school on the benefits of being in the Army to one of the senior English classes. The teacher was pro-military and she invited me to talk about my military experiences. Whenever I did a presentation, I wore my full dress blue uniform. There was an ultimate sense of pride when I wore it. It was snappy and one could not help but feel proud with this suit of armor.

Upon completing the classroom presentation, I headed down the hallway to the teachers' parking lot where I was allowed to park my vehicle. As I walked down the hallway, I noticed an older, short gentleman walking towards me. From afar, I could see that he was looking at me but not really seeing me. As he got closer, he began to look more and more familiar, but I couldn't quite place his face or from where I knew him.

As he came upon my left shoulder, he gave me a courteous smile where I noticed his teeth. They were stained brown and yellow and I knew I had seen them before.

As he passed behind me, I stopped dead in my footsteps. I turned around and did a double-take. It was him! It was Mr. McGowan, my college chemistry professor/molester.

I wanted to tell him to stop and turn around. I wanted him to look at me and acknowledge me. I wanted him to bow down to me and beg me for my respect. I wanted him on his knees begging for mercy and for his life. Again, I found myself wanting something that was not going to happen. I watched him walk away, but he didn't disappear down the long corridor. Instead, he turned into the same room that I had just come out of where I had just given my presentation to the English class.

The pro-military teacher of this English class was Mrs. McGowan, who thought the world of me! It hit me like a pile driver! Mr. McGowan and Mrs. McGowan were husband and wife! I never put that connection together. Mrs. McGowan was the sweetest lady in the world. She couldn't possibly be married to a child molester!

Again, I found myself in a position of complete power. I felt that I now owned this individual's soul and everything in his material life. I could ruin his life forever. I returned the next day to follow up with Mrs. McGowan.

Between classes, I poked my head in and asked Mrs. McGowan if she had a few minutes to give me some feedback on the presentation. She said I could visit anytime for any reason and it was a good time since she didn't have a class to teach for the next period. We briefly discussed the students' feedback and she thanked me for enlightening her students.

Changing the subject, I told her that I ran into Mr. McGowan in the hallway the previous day and wondered if that was her husband. She smiled and said *yes, we've been married for over 35 years.*

I explained to her that he was my Chemistry professor a few years back. I asked her to tell him that *Tony Ladron de Guevara* said "Hi".

He'd remember my last name since he had such a hard time pronouncing it during roll call.

She mentioned how small a world we lived in and the six degrees of separation theory. I told her I agreed and would love to take them both out to dinner one day. She insisted that she would rather have me over for dinner at their house and I exclaimed what a great idea that would be. I'd look forward to it. She had no idea just how forward I did look to having dinner at their house!

I imagined myself showing up for dinner at their house and reminding her husband about how great it was to have him as my Chemistry teacher. The questions I would ask him at the dinner table in front of his wife would be endless; *Do you have children? They must really be proud of you being a college professor and all. How do you feel about people who abuse their authority that are in public positions of trust? Oh I don't know, like child molesters for example? What should our society do with people like that when they are convicted?*

I sat quietly, but the questions and comments that I could make at that dinner table flooded my brain.

I asked Mrs. McGowan to consult with her husband to pinpoint a date and time and I would be there. I would have paid a mint to be a fly on the wall to see the reaction on his face. The dinner invitation was never confirmed. I don't know how much mental anguish, if any, Mr. McGowan went through. I'm sure for the next few days, maybe weeks, he feared for his livelihood. In my mind, he was just biding his time and waiting for me to tell his wife everything. Whether he did or not, it gave me some semblance of vengeance for what he did to me and the scar he left on my soul. I thought to myself at the time; *May he rot in Hell for what he did to me and what he may have done to others.*

1ST MARRIAGE – EMPTY CHURCH

Prior to Desert Storm, I had been seriously dating a girl for several years. We had a lot of ups and downs, but she stuck by me through thick and thin. At this point, in 1989, Desert Storm was being initiated. I was assigned to the 7th Infantry Unit in Ft. Ord and my unit was on the list to be deployed.

In case of our demise, we were told to prepare our last Will and Testaments, and any other last minute things that were needed prior to leaving for war. It was rather sobering to think that some, even all, of us may not come back. There was also the thought that some of us who returned may come back with missing limbs or as victims of biological warfare.

With this in mind, I thought if there were any time to get married, now was the time to do it. At least my new wife would have medical, dental, commissary and PX privileges in my absence. In the event of my death, she would be entitled to lifelong benefits. With talks of imminent war, we didn't have a lot of time and could only plan a small wedding with immediate family and friends. Invitations were sent to our parents and closest family and friends.

The church we chose had a very typical cathedral-like setting. There were stained glass windows and a step-up alter as one would find in a traditional church.

When I faced the back of the church waiting for my soon-to-be wife to come up the aisle, I wasn't surprised at what I saw. My fiancée's side of the church was filled with guests while on my side sat one single person: Mr. Sanchez.

While it was expected, it was still disheartening and embarrassing. I felt a knot in my stomach. What should have been yet another day to share with my parents, turned out to be just another disappointment. I should have expected it but thought this day would be the exception.

I looked at Mr. Sanchez and waved. I mouthed the words, "Thank you." He smiled and gave me a nod of approval. It meant the world to me.

Desert Storm only lasted 100 hours. My unit was on stand down mode and we never had to deploy. While we all were nervous, we were anxious to use all the training that was given to us for such an event. It's what we signed up for and what we trained daily to do. Most of us were disappointed, but I gained a beautiful wife out of the deal.

Unfortunately, like many others that I thought I could trust or felt were closest to me, I would be disappointed. My wife and best friend became closer to each other than to me. My marriage barely lasted one year.

COMMUNITY HOSPITAL – MONTEREY PENINSULA

In 1992, after serving ten years in the Army, I felt I wasn't living up to my full potential. Regardless of the retirement benefits for another ten years of service, I felt that the additional time needed to retire would have been wasted. I wanted more out of life than resigning myself to an early retirement check.

In time, I ended up getting a job working in the Emergency Room at the local Community Hospital. My job was to assist in patient triage, registration, take their vitals and get them admitted as needed. While there were many things that I witnessed in that emergency room that would make most people sick to their stomachs, there was only one thing that bothered me. It was the look of fear that I knew and understood so well. It was the look a child gives to a parent when they are in complete fear of what would happen next.

It was my job to ask questions about the patients' medical history and the nature of their visit. Oftentimes, we'd ask the child directly in those events where the parent wasn't there to witness the injury. I could tell when a child was fabricating a story in an attempt to correlate it to the injury.

In one case, a six-year-old had come into the E.R. with two black eyes. He said that he hit his eye on the doorknob. When I asked him about the other eye, he quickly looked up at his mother to help with his story.

She responded, "He's clumsy and did it to other eye as well."

I wanted to reach across the desk and choke the truth out of her. I knew from my EMT medical training those two black eyes, referred to as *raccoon eyes* in medical slang, and was usually a result of blunt force trauma to the head.

Shoulder injuries were common among abused children. Angry parents would lift their kids straight up in the air by one arm and tear the rotator cuff or stretch the shoulder ligaments so badly that the child was in absolute agonizing pain. The story told to me, would usually be that their child was rough housing with other kids.

It was not my job to determine if their stories were true or not, but I knew that look in the children's eyes. It was the look they'd give to their parents to see if they did well with the story they were telling. It ripped my heart out to witness this.

In the end, I could only hope that the doctors would know the look and get the in-house social workers and CPS (Child Protective Services) involved where and when they felt it was needed. In many cases, there wasn't enough proof to substantiate a child abuse allegation. In my heart of hearts, however, I could feel that child's pain and knew that their injuries were not due to 'accidents'.

6

Monterey CPS Contract (1995)

I N 1995 I ended up getting a herniated L-4 and L-5 discs after attempting to place a heavy patient on a gurney by myself. Pursuing a career in the medical field was no longer possible since lifting patients was a required task. The herniation closed one door but opened another. My inert drive to start my own business and my new found affinity for computers compelled me to start my own computer consulting service.

The internet craze was just starting with *America Online* and the need for personal PC's was increasing tenfold. I started a business called *PC Consulting for Dummies* inspired by the Dummy books that are famous for teaching with simplicity.

While most of my friends said I was crazy for naming my business that had the implication my clients were dumb, I countered with "If they don't have a sense of humor about computers, then I don't want them as clients."

The business worked and I stayed busy.

One day, I received a call from a lady who identified herself as a County worker from the *Department of Child Welfare Services*. She stated that she had been referred to me by the local *Egghead Software* store where I had dropped my business cards off. She went on to say that the county was looking for a computer instructor who was interested in bidding on a contract to teach a new database system.

The short end of this story was --I succeeded in obtaining the contract. This was the one single event that catapulted me into an understanding of child abuse.

I never really realized that I was a victim until I read the reports that the social workers wrote after going out on investigations. In reading those reports, I saw myself as that five-year-old from so many years ago. I wondered where my social workers were when I needed them.

After a couple of months I felt a bond to all the social workers in Monterey County. It was rewarding to be a part of a system where the sole purpose was to protect children. I admire them for what they do and often wonder how they are able to get through their own pain of seeing abused children.

High caseloads only add to their frustration. It's a thankless job in a society that seems to look upon them as *children snatchers or family busters*. The media never seems to have anything positive to say about them and the attention always seems to focus on the negative cases that will get viewer ratings. Unfortunately, in our twisted society, that means reporting the stories of the children that died or fell through the system – not the success stories.

THE SEARCH FOR MY BIRTH MOM BEGINS

The new database I was hired to teach also incorporated part of a system utilized by adoption workers. Monterey County was one of the first counties to be trained. This became the first page of my search for my biological mother. I now had a starting point to consult with social workers that dealt with adoptions on a daily basis. They would have the knowledge and resources to aid me in my quest. I consulted with one of my students, Beth Foley, who was a supervisor for the Adoptions Unit.

I asked her what I needed to do to initiate my search. She happily handed me some paperwork and a phone number for me to submit my waiver of confidentiality. She explained that at the very least, I would receive non-identifying information about my birth parents. If my mother had submitted her waiver, we then would be contacted and information would be exchanged to allow us to meet.

I remember feeling the apprehension and excitement of filling out the paperwork. On one side, I felt it was only a matter of submitting paperwork and we would be reunited. The other side kept reminding me to not set myself up for that type of expectation.

I called the number Beth had given me. It was the direct number to the office my waiver was being remitted to.

It was explained to me how the process of re-unification worked. It was pretty simple. If my birth mother submitted her waiver, she would be contacted by mail with my name, phone number, and address. If not, all I would receive was the non-identifying information. This consisted of information such as medical history, ethnicity, and any information that was available at the time of my birth that would not identify who my mother actually was. Even with that, it was more than I knew and I would be closer to her spiritually.

The next couple of months seemed to drag. I checked the mail every day after I sent the waiver in. Even after I was told it would take up to six months due to backlogs, I checked daily for the next three months. I was like a child a week before Christmas morning.

Finally in July, an official looking envelope from the *Children's Home Society* arrived in my mailbox. My heart started to beat like a drummer on a triple shot of espresso. My breathing became shallow and my hands perspired as if they were encased in a jungle dense, mini solarium. I wanted to be alone so I waited until I got home. I sat down, slowly opened the envelope and then the letter. It read:

Dear Mr. Ladron de Guevara,
At this time we regret to inform you that there is no waiver on file...

That was all I had to read.

A feeling of complete remoteness and obscurity seemed to engulf my soul. I sat there for a long time wondering if I ever would find my real mom. I wanted to know what she looked like, how she smiled and how she hugged. Any hope that I had at this point seemed to fizzle like a miner's lamp on its last drop of kerosene.

THE SEARCH INTENSIFIES (1998)

After developing the curriculum and training for Monterey County, a representative from *IBM Global Services* called me and offered me a training consultant contract to continue the statewide implementation and training development.

With this new opportunity the search for my biological mother intensified in both method and desire. State project headquarters was located in Sacramento, and this is where, as a baby, I was placed for adoption.

It felt strange to return to that city. It felt like home for me. I had this strange notion that my mother was somewhere in this city. I felt closeness to her like I had never felt before.

The classes I was going to teach were being held in Sacramento and I had to report to work on Monday morning. To avoid the morning rush, I left on Sunday night.

I drove into downtown trying to find a hotel. Somehow I meandered my way down Capitol Street from J Street. As I looked down the street, in front of me was the State Capitol. It was mesmerizing. The lights on the building seemed to cast a magnificent glow – like an angelic halo of sorts. Somewhere in this city I felt that there was a connection. For me, this was ground zero. It was as though some magnetic draw brought me to this city. I was given life here. This was home. This is where I felt a connection.

During my assignment to IBM, I would spend five days a week living at the Residence Inn.

To pass idle time I would go to *Arden Fair Mall* which was down the street from the class I was teaching. *Barnes and Noble* was my favorite hangout and I often found myself looking into the faces of strangers wondering if there was a connection: a blood connection. Maybe, just maybe, one of these people was related to me - a brother, sister, cousin or an aunt. Little did I know that I was actually much closer than I realized.

My students consisted of clerical workers and administrative personnel at all levels of social work in child protective services. These also included social workers in adoption services. The computer database application was extensive and it was intimidating for most students who were accustomed to an outdated paper and folder method of record keeping.

In order to break the ice, I would always start my classes by sharing the story of my adoption (sans the abuse) and my current search for my biological mother. This never failed to develop a bond with my students. It showed that I was just as human as they were and not some robotron teacher of computers.

One day, one of my students stayed after class. She gave me a phone number that she said would help in my search process. She claimed she had just found her own biological mother only a few weeks prior and the investigator in her case was more than she could have imagined.

I looked at the number and was surprised at the area code of the phone number. The area code was my own! She said the investigator was from Salinas.

I thought to myself, "Coincidence or fate?"

I thanked her and she wished me luck. She told me that her reunion was phenomenal and it changed her life forever. There was a look of peace and happiness in her face. It was the look and feel that I, too, wanted to have.

Later that week, I called the number and spoke to the investigator. Richard was very cordial. He asked me my motive for searching. I replied simply with "Grounding."

I explained the void I felt of not knowing where I came from or who I came from. I'm not sure if he would have taken my case had I answered any differently. He seemed genuinely concerned about my ability to handle the situation whatever the outcome.

I gave him what little information I had about my adoption. Richard said it wasn't a lot, but it was a start. He would call me if anything developed or if he needed any additional information. In the interim, I would have to be patient and contact him with the non-identifying information that I was still waiting to receive from *Children's Home Society*.

THE COURT DOCUMENT

In spite of all the disparities I had with my adoptive mom, I still attempted to maintain some sort of open line of communication with her. Four years had passed since I last saw her. We seemed to have developed a pattern of arguments that would last over a period of years. Each one of us would hold out as long as possible before attempting to speak to the other. After a while we couldn't remember what we argued about and I would end up conceding.

This time I had a specific motive for returning home. After landing my contract with IBM, I was finally making the income I had always aspired to make and be in a position that allowed me freedom and independence.

Now was my opportunity to tell her how wrong she had always been. I am somebody. I did amount to something. I am important. Despite everything she tried to tell me when I was younger, I was here to tell her she was a liar.

There was something very therapeutic in telling her of my success. In doing so, subliminally, I was telling her "Fuck you!" all over again. I felt redemption, but it wasn't complete. It wasn't enough. I wanted something more. I wanted an apology, an apology that didn't come and never will.

What I did get, however, was a vital piece of my life. Mom had no idea that I had initiated a search for my biological mother.

After dinner, she told me to sit down. She said she had something she wanted to give to me.

She left for a couple of minutes and returned with paperwork that looked old but appeared to be some sort of legal document.

"We've wanted to give these to you for a long time, but didn't think it was time until now."

She handed the documents to me and told me they were the original court documents for the finalization of my adoption. This was the very document that they had shown me the night they told me I was adopted! It was my adoption decree!

At that moment every ounce of air left my lungs. I immediately scanned the document for anything that linked me to an identity other than the one I was raised with.

There it was! On the second page: "James Christopher Improgo." My birth name! I had something! I looked harder. Where was her name? I couldn't find it. Dammit! To protect her confidentiality, they didn't record it.

Nonetheless, it was a start.

My last name screamed ethnicity! It wasn't Smith or Johnson or a name for which it was difficult to figure out ethnic origin. It was *Improgo*. It was tangible. It had identity. I had identity!

My head spun. Hundreds of thoughts went whirling through my mind. What ethnicity could *Improgo* be? It didn't sound Indonesian like my mom had been telling me all those years. Then again, what exactly was an Indonesian name?

"Are you going to try and find her now?"

I immediately came out of my daze.

She symbolically handed me a knife when she handed me those court documents. Her question became the knife pointing precariously above her heart. I was the bearer of that knife. If there was any opportunity to exact the vengeance that I so longed for, this was it.

I could say *yes* and then twist it in deeper by saying *Now I can find my real mother and love someone who will love me like a real son!*

Even with all those years of lingering pain, I just could not do it. I couldn't tell her. No matter what she did or said to me, she was still my mom. I didn't want her to feel the pain that I endured from her for so many years. I protected her with a lie.

"No Mom. You are my only mother and I have no desire to search."

A look of relief came over her. I told her *thank you* for the documents and that I would make a copy for keepsake and nothing more.

Hugging and saying "I love you" was not something that was done in this family. Material gifts were ways of expressing positive emotion in our family. So for Mother's Day I bought her an Italian leather living room set. It was the only way I knew how to express my gratitude to her.

The document she gave me would change my life infinitely.

After my instructing assignment was completed, I was re-assigned to the *Los Angeles Department of Child and Family Welfare Services*. My role was now changed to end-user support and assisting with application rollouts for the offices that were coming onboard. It was there I met a very animated, extremely likable, social worker. Her name was Joi Russell, and she was going to be my new interim boss.

Her presence was one that commanded everyone's attention. She had all the personality traits I found admirable in a person. When she walked into the room, everyone knew it. She was a people person. Her smile was contagious and her sense of humor kept everyone on their toes. It was the kind of presence I wanted to achieve with others. She was a seasoned social worker, very knowledgeable and had many resources at her fingertips.

After receiving my court documents, I consulted with her about the ethnicity of my birth name of *Improgo*. I explained my situation for wanting to know and she started to ask me questions about my quest. Her questions asked by anyone else would probably have been too personal, even intrusive, but I felt comfortable opening up to her.

She explained a similar situation with a relative who also had been searching and the rollercoaster of events and emotions that transpired with them. She was assessing me as a social worker would, to see if I was emotionally prepared for any events that were about to happen. She asked me about the things that drove me to do what I do.

After I answered her, she explained that I sounded almost identical to someone who authored a book about his own search for his biological mother. She told me she would send me the book and that it would give me some insight into why I was the way I was.

A couple of weeks later, I received a book in the mail titled "A Man and His Mother" by Tim Greene.

It was the one gift that had such a quintessential impact on my own introspection of who I was as an adoptee.

In reading this book, I didn't feel alone anymore. I was no longer an outsider looking in. There was someone else who was in my age group that felt the emotions I felt. In all the times I heard, "I know how you feel" from non-adoptees, it was the author of this book that could truly feel it.

Unless a person is an adoptee, no one can truly understand the void we have in our lives. There is no grounding, no starting point, and no ending until we have the physical connection to our biological relations.

Does this imply that all adoptees have the desire to search for their biological parents? The answer to that is simply *no*. Many adoptees are content with how their lives developed and the relationships therein. However, it is believed that when the adoptee suffers from a significant loss, such as a loved one, or other traumatic event, this desire to know is set into motion.

In my case, the desire to know my biological mother did not factor in until my adolescent years. I believe it was at this point in my life that I came to the full realization that the way I was raised is not how a real mother would treat her child. This was my trauma. True or not, I knew I had to find my biological mother one day. Although it was drilled into my head that I would amount to nothing, a nobody, I would only present myself to my birth mother as something; a somebody.

During this time period, many thoughts crossed my mind. What if I never find her? What if I do and she doesn't want to see me? What if I was a product of a rape? How would I handle that? Could I handle that?

I had to face the real possibility that perhaps my birth mother wouldn't want to have anything to do with me or even that I may never find her and live my life in a wanton void. Would not knowing who she was be more painful than finding her and having her not wanting anything to do with me? My mind spun with these questions but never deterred me in my desire to know. It was an obsession. I had to know something; anything. Even if it were just a picture, that would be a life line to me.

During my search, I started to write letters to my mom to chronicle my feelings of desperation.

Dear Mom,

Thursday, April 01, 1998 - 9:47 am

Radisson Hotel, San Bernardino (lobby)

Today I've spent the last three hours on the Internet in hopes of finding you. I was hopeful that you might have found this an easier method of finding me as well. There were moments of sweating palms and skipped heartbeats, only to be disappointed when the search results came back nil.

It's been three months since I seriously began my search for you. I've hired a private investigator but to date I haven't heard anything. Questions run rampant through my mind more than ever before. I want to see you...talk to you...hug you. I want your validation and the smile that I know will come from it. I want you to be proud of me. I want you to know that I understand your reason for giving me up for adoption. I want to thank you for that decision. I want to thank you for giving me life. I know that there are many characteristics in me that I have inherited from you. I have passion and drive unlike most. I want only to be the best in all that I do. I don't settle for mediocrity. I am an achiever. I have achieved what most dream to achieve in a lifetime. I know this drive comes from you. I can feel it.

By the way, and I'm sure you probably know, you gave birth to me exactly 34 years ago.

June 10, 1998 - 4:52 p.m.

Dear Mom,

Today has been a very emotionally taxing day. My adoptive parents told me that you were a student at California State University at Sacramento at the time of my conception. I was there this afternoon to find anything about you that I possibly could. It felt strange to walk on the campus, buildings, and streets that you yourself may have walked thirty-four years ago. Needless to say my heart was pounding and my palms were sweating.

This was the closest I've ever come to you. I can't recall the last time I've felt so many emotions hitting me at one time. All the while it felt so surreal. So, so close, yet...At the very least I wanted to see or touch anything that had the name "Improgo" on it...but I must wait another day. I had to make an appointment with the head of archives. I'll meet with her tomorrow to go through the yearbooks for the period of time that you may have attended.

A simple confirmation would make me feel closer to you. A picture of you in the yearbook would be a gift. I envision you as a very beautiful, smiling, animated woman. I know I could pick you out without even referencing the names. Your eyes and your smile would be my clues.

Disappointingly there were no new discoveries today. Tomorrow is another day however. Hopefully tomorrow I'll be another step closer to you.

DISENCHANTED

As the days passed without results, time seemed eternal. It felt as though my void was becoming deeper and darker and there would be no light to be shed into it. What I thought would be my saving grace might turn out to be my demise. Without knowing who or where my mother was, it began to feel as though my birth certificate only widened and deepened my emotional chasm. The adage of *so close, but so far away* seemed to poke its ugly head through my blackened walls.

More questions came to mind. Am I chasing my own tail? Am I setting myself up for more disappointment? Were all these emotional ups, but more downs, worth the anguish?

These questions crossed my mind for a minute and only lasted for that time period. I would search until I could no longer search and/or until it was time to leave this big blue spinning marble. Giving up was not an option no matter how I felt. I had to pick myself up and keep pushing and finding other means or resources.

It was a couple of weeks before I heard from Richard, so when I saw his number come across my pager, my heart felt as though it were going to explode out of my chest.

As a retired police officer, Richard had many resources that the public at large could not access. He explained that he combed through as many databases as he could to find the last name of *Improgo*. With this, he sent out letters to everyone in his database with that last name. Fortunately, he explained, there were only a couple of hundred due to the uniqueness of the last name.

The letter explained that he was an investigator that was trying to reunite an adopted son and his biological mother. He further explained that the confidentiality of the mother would be kept and no information would be shared without her expressed permission. He was only on a fact finding mission and would respect any wishes or concerns the mother would have. Finally, any type of information from a third party would be greatly appreciated and the confidentiality would obviously be extended to them.

As I listened in excitement to Richard's brilliant approach, my excitement was squashed when he said he received a couple of interesting replies but none that were helpful to my case. He didn't elaborate on the interesting replies and apologized to me that there wasn't much else he could do and that he exhausted his means.

When he said that, I felt as though all the oxygen was squeezed out of my lungs. It was that sinking feeling of despair that this was the final straw. There was nothing else he or I could do. I was at a dead-end and my biggest fear was realized. I would live my life on this earth with no grounding or feeling of being connected.

I was a stray puppy with nowhere to go and no warmth to feel from his mother. I was on my own and would have to survive with never knowing who or where my mother was. My tail was tucked and I felt like cowering into a corner and just whimpering myself to sleep. I acquiesced to the fact that the situation *was what it was*. I did the best I could with the information I had, but I was still determined to find her.

LEARNING ABOUT OTHER ADOPTEES

After teaching classes, I'd find myself poking around on internet adoptee forums. This gave me a chance to chat with others that were going through similar situations or were actually successful in finding their biological families. Some stories were out of a fairy tale book with happy endings, but many others were not as happy and some were even disastrous.

There were scenarios of sibling or other relative rivalry as well as accusations of ulterior motives, such as trying to claim future family inheritances. It seemed to be a sad commentary on what some people place value on.

It goes without saying that the true colors, be it bright or dark, seem to come out in all of these adoptee reunions. Other scenarios that did not fare well, were situations where family members were never told of the child that was put up for adoption. In many cases, this resulted in a non-supportive or non-acceptive family. They felt lied to and that their trust was violated. In some cases, the end result was divorce or years of marriage counseling. It's plausible that there may have been other matters in the relationship. With the adoptee showing up, deeper issues that were just under the surface may have triggered them to quickly rise to the surface. Every reunification scenario has its own set of circumstances and therefore an adoptee shouldn't set any expectations if/when they are reunited with their biological families.

When I went into chat rooms on this subject, the chats were eye opening, educational, and sometimes heated with differences in opinion.

All things considered, for those who did find their *bios* (biological families) and asked if they would do it again, the answer always seemed to be a resounding yes; no matter what the outcome turned out to be. The common thread of *needing* to know *their roots* seemed to be most prevalent.

THE PHONE CALL

That summer seemed to be overwhelmingly hot. I couldn't acclimate to the dry heat of Sacramento. This was especially true after living in Monterey Bay for nine years. The Sacramento summer heat seems to be on the opposite spectrum of the cool Monterey Bay spring-like summers and summer-like autumns.

When I let my class out for lunch, I tried not to venture too far away from the classroom to pick up something to eat. As a matter of profession, I would always be in a tie and long sleeved shirt and tried not to spend more time outside than I had to in the sweltering heat. This would also give me time to get back to my classroom and prepare for the next lecture before the early students returned for additional help.

I returned from lunch early and sat down to prepare for the afternoon lessons. I was suddenly startled by the vibration of my pager. I looked down and saw that it was Richard calling.

As in every instance that he paged, my heart began to race. I went into the Administrator's office and picked up a phone at an empty cubicle. My hands began to perspire and my breathing became shallow. As I dialed his number, I thought everyone in the building could hear my heart beating.

When Richard picked up my call, in a very calm voice, he said "Tony, I found your mother."

If I hadn't been standing in front of a chair during that phone call, I would have hit the floor square on my backside. My knees seemed to become disjointed, so I slowly buckled into the chair.

"Are you sure it's my mom?" I blurted out.

"Yes, I am positive." he replied.

"Does she want to see me?"

"In the beginning, she wasn't sure. When I explained why you wanted to find her, she said *yes.*

Every emotion that a person could possibly feel, I felt in the next thirty seconds. I was excited, scared, anxious, happy, and overwhelmed all in one instant. There are not enough words in the English dictionary to explain all the things I felt in that moment. If *Webster* were a re-unified adoptee, I wondered how many more words would have been created to characterize his feelings.

I asked how he found her and he explained;

"Well, when your mother got married, she took on her new married name of *Fredericks*. Since the letters were only sent to those with the last name of *Improgo*, your mother did not receive one. A gentleman (who turned out to be my Uncle Greg) received the letter in Daly City and forwarded it to your mom in Washington simply as a matter of interest. He had no idea that his sister was your mother! She called me upon receiving the letter and her story matches yours. I confirmed other things that only she would know. This is definitely your mother. Here's her phone number. She wants you to call her tomorrow when you can. Best of luck, Tony."

I was dumbstruck. I could scarcely utter the words *thank you* as I hung up the phone. I couldn't move from where I sat and my mind was in a spin, yet again.

As many times as I thought of what I'd say to her, I kept thinking to myself, "What will I say to her? What will she say back? Is she going to be happy to hear from me? Oh my god! I'm going to talk to my mother for the first time in my life! What type of impression am I going to make? How is all this going to turn out?"

As my mind kept spinning, I shuffled back to my classroom. I was in a daze as I sat at the corner of my desk looking at the floor. I couldn't hear or see anything other than what was in my mind's eye. It was like being on auto pilot during a long drive. It's similar to when you are driving and in deep thought, and in the end you wonder how you got to your destination. This was my state of mind.

When I snapped out of it, I looked at the clock on the wall and it was 1:20 p.m. Class starts at 1:00 p.m. sharp. I looked around the classroom and all eyes were on me; the students were silent. One of them quietly said to me, "Tony, are you okay?"

Since I am a very animated and energetic trainer, my students knew that something was wrong. They all knew my adoption search story as I always thanked them for doing what they did for a living. During breaks, many of them wanted me to share my feelings and thoughts from the perspective of a child victim turned adult. It helped them to better understand child abuse from the first person's perspective.

I looked around the room slowly to make eye contact with everyone in the room. I answered the question very calmly, "I found my mom."

With that announcement, half the room erupted in cheers and ap-plause while the other half cried with joy. Everyone was affected. They had many questions and concerns about my feelings and thoughts. I told them that I was overwhelmed and wasn't feeling one certain thing; I was feeling many things.

I know they all wanted me to continue to talk about my feelings and as much as I wanted to, I still had a class to teach and we had to move on.

I'm not sure how I managed to teach that day. More importantly, after that revelation, I don't know if the students *learned* anything that day. When I looked at them, they all seemed to be distant and lost in their own thoughts.

7

Talking to My Birth Mom
for the First Time

I DIDN'T SLEEP MUCH that night. The anticipation of talking to my birth mom for the first time was incredible. I spent most of the night writing down all my thoughts and questions. I put myself in her shoes and tried to imagine how she was going to feel. She had to have been much more nervous than I. I'm sure she must have felt that I harbored some amount, if not a great deal, of resentment towards her. I knew I would have to set the stage for this conversation to put to rest any possibilities of uneasiness. I just wanted to tell her how much, over the years, I thought of her and that I had no expectations. I simply wanted to know who I was and where I came from.

The next day, after class, I called the number that Richard had given me. A man with a very calming and slow voice picked up the phone.

"Hi, is my mom there?"

"This must be Tony. She's been expecting your phone call all day. She became very anxious and went to play bingo to calm her nerves," he chuckled.

"Is this her husband?"

"Yes, my name is Marvin. You can call me Marv. I've known about you ever since I met your mom. She always thinks about you."

At that point, I just wanted to cry, but I had too many questions.

"Can you tell me how she is, what happened, what's my ethnicity, why was I put up for adoption, when did she make the decision, where is..."

It was probably the longest run-on sentence/question in the *Guinness Book of World Records.*

He politely cut me off and said, "Those are questions that I feel your mom would best answer."

He was right and I was just too anxious to wait.

"Call back at eight o'clock tonight. She'll be home by then."

I told him that I would and thanked him.

I was afraid to hang up the phone in fear that I would lose the connection forever.

At 7:29 p.m. and 59 seconds, I was dialing the last digit of my birth mom's phone number. My heart was fluttering faster than a hummingbird's wings on a warm spring day.

As the phone began to ring, I began to feel that this was all a dream. It seemed surreal that after so many years I was about to talk to my real mom. I felt very nervous. Whichever way this conversation was about to go, I knew I was at the helm of this boat. It was up to me to steer it in a positive direction. When she picked up the phone, I took a deep breath.

As soon as I heard her say *hello*, I knew it was her. I detected an accent, but couldn't pinpoint its possible country of origination.

"Mom? This is your son, Tony."

She responded softly "I know son."

She called me son! My mom called me son!

That one word from her elevated me to a level that I never knew. I could feel the tension, yet the relief in her voice.

"The first thing that I would like to say to you is *thank you* for doing something unselfish so that I could have the life I have."

I heard her let out a deep sigh of relief, but still sensed the tension. I knew I had to make her feel more at ease.

"I have so many questions, but there is one question that has been at the forefront of my mind for all these years."

I could hear her taking a deep breath in anticipation of the question.

"Yes? What is your question, son?"

"Mom…" I paused consciously with my own deep breath, "is there premature balding in the family?" I blurted out.

We both laughed and I felt the cloud of tension lift over our heads. Something as simple as sharing a laugh with my mom for the first time is inexplicable. It was an instant bonding and my void was quickly filling up. The dark tunnel that was negated of sound and feeling was now filling with the laughter and light that seemed to emanate through the phone line from my mom. It was simple laughter, but it was so much more than that on so many different levels.

"No son, you have no worries," as she continued to laugh. "I see you have inherited the funny gene from the family."

Up until a minute ago, I never gave thought to inheriting genetics. I now have traceable genes! What an incredible thing to have! Genes and a family to inherit them from! Those things that most people take for granted are gifts from heaven to me. Even now, it is difficult for me articulate these feelings.

"Okay Mom, here's the actual question I've been wanting to know; what is my ethnicity?"

"Well son, your dad was Caucasian and I was born in the Philippines."

"Hmmm…Caucasian and Filipino? That makes me a Cacapino…!"

More laughter ensued and the dialog just seemed to flow naturally from there.

The more we talked, the more complete I began to feel. I now had roots, grounding, family, history, and ethnicity. I also had siblings; two brothers and a sister!

We talked and talked for what seemed like hours. Mom explained that she came from a very devout *Catholic* family. In fact, so devout that two of my aunts were nuns, one of which was a *Carmelite* and the other a *Franciscan* nun.[10] While growing up, they were always surrounded by nannies that took care of and protected them. Her mom was a business savvy entrepreneur, and dad, a dentist who owned a pharmacy in the city of Bacolod (where my mom was born).

She came to America to pursue her Master's degree in Economics at *San Francisco State University* but ended up working in Anaheim for the phone company. Mom met a young man by the name of John at the *Palms Bar and Restaurant* and the two became enamored with each other. He was, blonde, intelligent, over six feet tall and an engineer. He was married but said he was separated. Knowing that he was still married, Mom said she didn't fall in love, and after discovering she was pregnant,

Mom graduated from the College of the Holy Spirit in the Philippines with a Bachelor's Degree in Economics

came back to Sacramento without telling him that she was with child.

In a family of devout Catholics, Mom couldn't tell the family for fear of rejection and humiliation. As a result, she found her way to the *Camellia House* on J Street in Sacramento; a women's shelter for unwed mothers. From there she was referred by a catholic nun where she stayed under the care of an elderly couple. When it was time, she gave birth to me at a local general hospital. She said she was only able to hold me for a brief moment and I was taken away to be placed for adoption.

From this story, it seemed uncanny how I had such a draw to want to attend Stanford University

---

10 The Carmelite sister leads a contemplative life, a considerable portion of her time being devoted to Divine service, meditation and other pious exercises, the rest occupied with household work and other occupations. The life is necessarily strict, the fasting severe, and there are many opportunities for exercising virtue. They are rarely seen in public as they are sequestered behind convent gates.

to become a business major and then had a career in the medical field. Was this simply a coincidence or was there a genetic imprint left on me as a result of what my mom and her parents did in their educational and career fields?

I didn't want to stop talking with her, but it got late and we had been on the phone for a while. We promised to speak to each other and/or write as much as we possibly could. I told her that I'd come over to visit as soon as I could get a break in my teaching schedule.

In that phone call, the big hole in my life was finally filled. I felt different. I felt whole. I was a real person.

Mom in 1963

FIRST LETTER TO MOM

July 4, 1998

Mabuhay [11] *Mom!*

I have so much that I would like to share with you and simply do not know where to start. I suppose the beginning is as good as any:

A very loving and caring couple adopted me at the age of 6 months. My father, who is of Mexican descent, was in the Army at the time. He had met my mother while he was stationed in Japan. My mother, who is first generation Japanese, was working at the military base and well, history was made.

My mother, due to internal complications, was unable to have children. It was decided that they would adopt. It was told to them at the adoption agency that your wish was to have me brought up in a good Catholic family. That wish came to fruition. I was baptized in a Catholic Church and attended catechism. As we traveled quite extensively, Catholic school was not an option while we were overseas. However, Sunday Mass was always in order.

As far back as I can remember I was always a child that wanted to stand out among the rest. I wanted to always be the first, the best, or the focus. Being the President of classes or organizations always seems to have been my calling. I can remember reciting a Christmas poem at a school function at the age of seven. I was the only one in my class that volunteered to do this solo. The rest of the children were too frightened to stand in front of an auditorium filled with parents and family members. Although I was scared, I recited this very long poem and received a standing ovation. I believe this type of reception and validation was the catalyst to pursuing those things that brought back those feelings of acceptance.

---

11 Tagalog for *hello.*

It was only a couple of years before this that my parents had told me that I was adopted. I can remember this day very clearly. I didn't quite understand the situation, but I do remember crying. It was presented to me in a very loving and caring fashion, but at the age of five, a child only understands acceptance or rejection. As I grew older, I began to understand more and accepted the fact that you only did this out of unselfish love for me.

As I was always competitive in all that I pursued, my mother expected nothing less than the best of me. She was always supportive and kept me in line when I deviated. She was strict but fair. Most of all she was proud. I excelled in academics as well as athletics. Again, I always had to be the focus and played pitcher or quarterback when it came to sports. In student government, I settled for nothing less than class president. I even became the President of the Filipino club. How ironic that no one, to include myself, thought that I was of Filipino descent but still voted me into this position.

I graduated in the top 5% of my class in high school as an Ephebian and was also the class salutatorian. I thought of you on many occasions, but I thought of you more on this day and wish I could have looked out into the crowd to see your proud face. I know you would have been.

I wanted to attend Stanford University but funding for college was not available. I did not want to burden my parents with such an exorbitant bill. I elected to join the military in order to fund my own college education. I became a Sergeant at the age of 20, which in itself was a major accomplishment. I ended up staying in longer than I anticipated and fortunately the war in the Gulf was over before I was ordered to go there.

Since this will probably end up being a very long letter, I would like to send this one as soon as possible. I only get to come home for the weekends. I will continue this letter as time permits. I have much more to tell and many questions to ask.

I will make more copies of this picture and will send it to you as soon as it is finished. For now, all I have was this scanned picture that I copied through my computer. I enjoyed conversing with Mr. Fredericks. He seems to be a kind and caring soul. I am glad to know that he took care of you. This was always my primary concern.

My only motive for finding you is to know that you were well and to let you know that I am forever thankful for your decision to put me up for adoption. I know that it was difficult and it was only for my benefit. I also had a strong desire to know what my heritage was. This was a very big void in my life. Yesterday I spent a good portion of my time studying about the Philippines and specifically the city of Bacolod on the island of Negros. I feel as though I have a whole new beginning in my life. I even bought a small desk flag of the Philippines for my office. I am very proud of my Pinoy ethnicity.

I would like to plan to visit with you. As a contractor, however, it is very difficult to schedule time off. I do not accumulate vacation time and will have to plan very far in advance. Maybe it would be possible just to visit for a weekend and catch up as much as we can? Please let me know what would be easiest for you. I am looking forward to your correspondence.

With Love and Thankfulness,
Claudio Antonio Ladron de Guevara Jr.
"Tony"

I didn't tell her the entire truth about the abuse at this point. It wasn't time. We had too much catching up to do and I didn't want to ruin any of it with bad news. It would have to wait. It wasn't until I started to write this book that I gave her a draft of the manuscript to read months later.

A Man and His Mother (Tim Greene) – Gift to Mom

July 7, 1998

Dear Mom,

The book enclosed was given to me as a gift from a social worker. In reading this book it was almost as if I were reading my own journal. The attributes and characteristics of this author are almost identical. I felt the same emotions drive and motivation as he does. It is quite uncanny. The constant need for validation seems to have started right after being told I was adopted. I believe this was my way of compensating for my feelings of rejection. More importantly, I knew that whenever I found you, I wanted to be presentable. I wanted to be at the pinnacle of my career so that I would receive the most important validation of all: yours.

The void in my life seems to be closed for now. This dark cloud that seemed to loom over me is now gone. I feel relieved. As I get to know you more, as well as the rest of my new family, I know I will still have one looming question. You probably already know that it will be about my biological father. It is not important to me at this juncture, but I know it will be later. At this point all I want to know is about you, your wonderful life, and our heritage.

I know it will be difficult for you to tell my siblings about me. I am extremely happy though, that you have decided to. I was an only child and had always wished for a brother or sister. That was the other void in my life. I can't expect that they will be accepting of me. I only pray that they will understand. I have no ill intention or agenda. I don't want to be intrusive or a detractor. I have no expectations. All I can do is be hopeful.

My career seems to have come full circle. The very people that I teach computers to are the ones that have assisted you in placing me with a good family. Almost daily I am among social workers that place children with adopting families. They have all given me emotional support on every level. When I received the phone call from Mr. Lee that he had located you, I was right in the middle of giving a class. My students applauded and were very happy for me. I must have repeated my story at least a hundred times this week.

I'm looking forward to your pictures and correspondence. I will write and call whenever I get the opportunity, okay?

Your Son with Love,

Tony

THE LETTER TO MY SIBLINGS

August 20, 1998

Dear James, Lisa, and Tommy,

I am writing this letter to the three of you. I must admit that all the emotions that one can feel I am feeling at one time. I am overjoyed at the prospect of having siblings that I always longed for as an only child. However, after consulting with other adoptees and their circumstances, I am fearful, that this joy will be short-lived, as the three of you may not accept me as part of the family. If this were true, I have to say that I can understand this from the perspective of the situation being reversed.

Many questions would run through my mind as they probably are running through yours. In brief they would be: When? How? Who, and Why? I cannot answer all of these questions. Our mother will probably best ascertain most of these. I can however attempt to allay any fears or concerns that you may have about my motives and intent.

My intent is not to take anything away from the three of you. The fact is that there could be nothing taken away from any of you, only added. I am not here as a replacement but rather as a supplement to what is already whole. I am of no greater value to our mother than any of you are to her. The only thing that I ask from all of you is a chance to get to know you and then letting fate take its course.

For as long as I can remember as a child, I always asked my adoptive mother if she would go out and purchase a brother or sister for me. Although, growing up as an only child had many benefits, I know that I would have traded all of them for a brother or a sister. Now after 34 years, I cannot express the wonderment of knowing that I am related to the three of you by blood. When I look at the pictures of all of you, I am in awe of the resemblances that we share. Until recently, I had no bloodline that I knew of. This un-knowing feeling is one that is difficult to express. I can only describe it as a void or emptiness. No matter how successful I felt in life, this void never allowed me to quite enjoy any of my accomplishments completely.

There is closure to this now. That longing feeling of not knowing is gone. In its stead, however, is a new beginning for me to know what is. We have a common bond of blood and genetics and in my heart I know we must share personality traits, goals, and achievements that only brothers and sisters could share.

Two weeks ago was my first experience in feeling the pride a sibling can feel for another when I watched James on ESPN. I yelled to myself "My brother is on TV!" Anyone who saw or heard me would have thought I was having a brief episode of insanity when I was running around the house frantically trying to find a VHS tape to tape on. Unfortunately, I was only able to tape the last five minutes of the race.

I went to work the next day and was telling all my co-workers about James and showing his picture to everyone. In doing so, I also flaunted pictures of Tommy and Lisa. It was unanimous from all that the family resemblances are in each one of us. This in itself is something that I have never heard in all my life. It was, and is, a great feeling. I also have a picture that looks very much like the younger version of

Tommy. I noticed different physical attributes that each one of us share. I thought to myself that if I had come out a girl, that I would have looked like Lisa.

In closing, I just want to reiterate that my intent is not to claim anything material or take away anything personal. I am not here to replace but only to add. Lastly, I do not want to be an imposition on anyone. In fact, if there is something that I can offer, I would be happy to do whatever I can with the means that I have for any of you. It is my hope that you will consider all that I have said with your hearts and prayer.

Very sincerely,

Tony

P.S. Please feel free to contact me by mail or my paging system at any hour of the day.

The Cultural Mystery Unveiled - The Marketing of a Baby

The timing of my adoption could not have been any better. I was fortunate as a baby of ethnicity to be placed in an adoptive home as quickly as I was. I am not sure where I was or with whom I was placed during my first six months of life. I can only presume that I was in foster care or a children's home during that time.

The reason I consider myself fortunate during that time was because I was not marketable. Children of ethnicity were not a sellable product. Caucasian newborns were what the adoption market commanded. It just so happened that this *mixed marriage* couple was looking for someone just like me. Now that's perfect market timing.

Babies, newborns and infants especially, are a prized commodity in the market of adoptions. The older a child gets, the less marketable they become. *Children's Home Society* (CHS) where I was fostered knew this. They also knew their history.

During W.W.II, the Japanese reviled the Filipinos. Filipinos were (and even today still are among the Japanese elders), considered third class citizens by the Japanese.

This history caused a major dilemma for CHS. If this adopting Japanese mother knew the true ethnicity of this child, they lose a customer; a very hard to find customer.

What were they to do?

A crash course in Geography 101 is in order. The Philippines falls within the sea borders of Indonesia. Indonesia covers a lot of countries.

CHS technically did not lie to my parents. When the question of my heritage was brought up, they told the truth; in part. The half-truth being; *the child you are about to adopt is half Indonesian. The other half is Caucasian.*

Brilliant! I was off to a happy home (or so they thought).

THE ABUSE CONTINUES (ACCUSATIONS)

One would think that once a child reaches adulthood, the abuse stops. While this may be true as far as the physical abuse is concerned, the mental abuse can continue ad infinitum. It seemed that no matter how old I was, I would still feel like a child and be treated as one.

After a cordial visit with my adoptive parents, I returned to Monterey only to find a long nasty voicemail on my home phone from my mom accusing me of stealing a skirt for my wife (my 2nd marriage).

She was absolutely convinced that I stole this item from her house. I was dumbstruck. Where does she get the idea that I would steal from her and especially her clothing? I knew at this point there had to be some sort of chemical imbalance with her. The accusation was baseless, senseless, and just downright outrageous.

In the voicemail, she continued the accusation with ranting about my wife's heritage; to the extent of calling her *that Korean bitch.* She wasn't very happy that I was married to a ½ Korean ½ Filipina woman. In her belief system and cultural upbringing, those two cultures were beneath her.

It was for this reason I had never intended for the two of them to meet. I found it extremely insulting for her to make such a derogatory remark about my wife, especially since she had never met her.

I called her back.

"I don't know what the hell you are talking about! I didn't steal a skirt from you. Are you crazy? More importantly, who the fuck do you think you are to call my house and call my wife a Korean bitch? Don't you ever talk about my wife again! She has done more for me in the short time we've been together than you have in my entire life! In fact, don't ever call me again!"

With this, I slammed the phone down and it would be several years before I made contact with her again.

8

Long Awaited Reunion

It would be a few months before my work schedule allowed me to take a vacation. The anticipation was incredible and I couldn't wait to meet my mother for the first time. The flight to Seattle seemed to take forever. When we finally touched down, I wanted to run off the plane to see her.

I had no idea what she looked like but had no problem picking her out of the crowd. I walked up to her and said "Mom?"

She replied with "Hi son!" and with that we gave each other a hug. I had to stoop down since she was all of 4'10" tall. She was tiny! I thought to myself that my father must have been a giant since I was a full foot taller than her. I thought I was going to crush her if I squeezed her too hard. I never had a hug such as this. This was my mother and this is how a mother hugs her child. It was such a great feeling.

Marvin, her husband, was the most gentle and laid back soul that I've ever met. He was soft spoken and seemed to be the opposite of my mom's feisty, energetic personality. He told me again that he knew of me as soon as he met my mom and supported her emotionally since the beginning. He said she never forgot about me and wanted to search for me, but the adoption agency told her it was illegal. From that day, Marvin always treated me like one of his own and I looked up to him as if he were my second dad.

On the drive to Silverdale, we talked about my brothers and sister and how they were looking forward to meeting me. She told me my brothers were very sports-oriented and were involved with extreme kayaking and rock climbing. We talked about everything we could during the ride home.

When we arrived at their home, my brothers and sister were waiting outside. The youngest of the brothers walked up to me and gave me a big, warm hug and said "Welcome to the family bro! I'm Tommy."

It was so cool that he greeted me like that. I looked at him and I saw many similar physical qualities we shared. I was completely blown away to see someone else that looked like me.

There's something very special about my little brother. He is the brother that I always wanted when I was younger. I feel very protective of him and there isn't a lot I wouldn't do for him.

For the first time in my life, I understood sibling bonding. I never understood as a child and always envied those that had it. When Tommy and I are together, I feel like I am getting another chance at my childhood. It must look pretty funny to see two grown men diving for pennies in a swimming pool or playing Guitar Hero on Xbox. We don't care. It's fun and he's my brother and it feels good to say that.

He looks up to me and asks me for life and business advice. To think someone values my opinion and looks up to me is a great feeling. I think the other reason I feel so attached to him is because I see that young man that once was me.

The next person to greet me was my sister, Lisa. We both seemed to be overjoyed at this reunion, "Welcome to the family, Tony!" And finally, James stuck out his hand and gave me a firm grip handshake. He seemed a little more reticent and I could understand his reservation. He was the oldest of the siblings and probably felt protective. I shook his hand back and said, "It's great to finally meet you James".

The house was a tree lined, two-story home on about an acre of land. It was very spacious and comfortable. The first thing I noticed was the Xbox in the living room. Apparently the boys had been playing before I got there. James asked if I played and I said 'of course!' So for the next several hours, James, Tommy and I were heavily involved in a James Bond game. It was as if we were trying to catch up on all our lost playtime.

Lisa sat back in awe and watched her adult brothers become little boys again. My mom would come out from the kitchen every so often to watch us. I could see the look of contentment on her face. She was very happy that her family was now complete. She spent most of that day in the kitchen preparing our first family dinner together. While Mom cooked, she sang in the kitchen. She just kept smiling and her eyes seemed to sparkle. The house smelled so good with different and exotic smells. I knew Mom was preparing some cultural Filipino dishes for me to experience.

When we all sat down for dinner, we bowed our heads to say grace. It was something that I had never experienced as a family, nor the bond that one feels when sitting at the table together as a complete and happy family. While my mom was the exotic cook of the family, Marvin was definitely the BBQ steak master of the West Coast. I must have put on ten pounds that night. It wasn't that I couldn't stop eating, I just didn't want to leave the table and the feeling of bonding that came with a family sit down dinner.

After dinner, the boys congregated around the Xbox again with Lisa looking on while Mom played the piano in the background. There was something about my mom's piano playing that seemed to mesmerize me. When she played 'Für Elise', I was floored.

James, Eric (my brother-in-law), Tommy, Lisa, and me

This tune was always a favorite piano piece for as long as I could remember. In fact, it was the ring tone on my cell phone and the first song I wanted to learn to play when I took piano lessons. When I shared this information with my mom, she smiled and said "When you were in my tummy, I would play this song for you all the time."

NEW RELATIVES AND A REVELATION

Before meeting my mom face to face, I had the opportunity to speak to one of my aunts on the phone.

> "Hi nephew!
>
> This is your Auntie Lidine. We are soooo happy to have you back in our family! Your mom and I are overjoyed! We cannot wait to meet you in person. I have to share a quick story with you. Your mom said she had great news to share with me but wanted to tell me in person. This, she told me, while I was on a pilgrimage in Lourdes, France[12]. While visiting the grotto, a stranger came to me and handed me a bouquet of red roses for no reason at all and walked away. When I turned around to thank her, she disappeared. When I met with your mom and she told me that you had found her, I thought that the roses were a sign from our Lord about you."

When I visited my Aunt Lidine's house for the first time, I had yet another epiphany. When I was teaching in Sacramento, I always felt my mom was close by. I couldn't explain the feeling, but it was more than just that. There was an energy that I felt that was present when I stayed at the *Residence Inn* on Howe Avenue. When I looked out into the backyard of my aunt's house, the hotel I stayed in was literally a stone's throw away from her house. When I told her and my mom, they both almost in unison

---

12 In 1858, a fourteen-year-old peasant girl named Bernadette Soubirous had a series of eighteen visions of the Virgin Mary who appeared in a niche in the grotto of Massabielle near Lourdes, a village on the Gave de Pau River in the foothills of the Pyrenees in southern France.

explained that my mom and Marvin had visited a couple of times while I was only a few hundred feet away! I couldn't believe it! I knew at that point that the feelings of my mom being close by were really true!

In time, I got to meet my uncles, aunts, cousins, in-laws, and their friends. It seemed so overwhelming. I wasn't used to all this attention and the family gatherings. It seemed to be the polar opposite of the sequestered family environment where I was raised. While growing up, I didn't experience many family get-togethers and those that I did attend always ended up with my adoptive parents fighting.

In time, I found myself passively pulling away from my newfound relatives. I believe that it comes from an emotional defensive mechanism that helps to protect me when people get too close to me on an emotional level. On a subconscious level, I avoid relationships when they get too close to my emotional comfort zone. I think this is a result of my history of abuse by those I was supposed to trust or were closest to me. I'm not a psychologist, but it seems to make logical sense to me.   Later in my life this was confirmed during a therapy session.

MOTHER'S DAY LETTER

May 3, 1999

My dearest Mom,

On this Mother's Day, I wanted to tell you how important you are to my life. There are no words in the dictionary to possibly convey how I feel. When you hug me, hold me, or say "I love you," there is warmth, comfort, and security that I have never felt before. When I am around you, your touches become my validation, your looks are my assurance, and your words are my solace. It is a peace I have searched for, for so many years and now I have that inner peace.

"The finest steel is forged by the hottest fires." My new cousin, Jory, told these words to me. Not knowing these exact words before, it is a philosophy that has shaped the person into which I have

become. I want you to know that even though life's fires were unbearable at times, I will always be grateful to you for giving me an opportunity to become that sword. It is because of the tempered steel that has formed me that I have been able to fight and win my life's battles. Most of those battles would have been lost by most, but I have been unfaltering. That is until now.

Even the densest of all metals has its melting point, including mine. In this case however, I yield to it happily. For it is the touch of your hand on mine, and the look of pride that you bestow upon me that turns this steel into water; water the very element that life depends upon to live. Thank you mom for allowing me that chance.

Your Man of Steel and Son Forever,

Tony

WRITING AND SHARING THE MANUSCRIPT

It would be months before I shared my *secret* with Mom. I wasn't sure how I was going to tell her that her unselfish plan to give me a better life through adoption didn't quite turn out the way she planned. I thought the best thing to do was to write everything down I could remember, put into chronological order and then give it to her. This way I could tell her the story without leaving anything out.

As I wrote more and more, I found myself remembering things that I didn't want to remember. The more I wrote, the more depressed I became. By writing down all the things I could remember, my mind was forced to extract the finer details of those events. I found that I had suppressed a lot of memories in a vault in the back of my brain. It was as if somehow my brain decided this information was unneeded or unwanted and simply chose to store it away in a deep recess of my mind.

The bottom line was; I had to relive those abysmal events all over again. Now, however, it was different. Rather than a child who lived it at the moment and then went off to the sandbox to play and forget about it, I was reliving each event as an adult. The brain now understands what is right and what is wrong based on new understanding, life experience, and education. It was now tougher to handle these replayed memories and I found myself in a deep depression. Self-blame questions started to come to my mind that I did not think about as a child:

Why did I allow that to happen?

Why didn't I seek help?

Why didn't anyone help me?

What did I do to trigger others' behavior towards me?

Was I really a bad child?

What did I do to deserve the abusive punishments?

The more I wrote, the angrier I became towards my adoptive parents. How could they do this? Why did my adoptive mom hate me so much? Why didn't my adoptive dad stop her? Why didn't he *man up* to her and tell her that he didn't believe in hitting me?

Along with the anger, also came relief. By writing all these events down, my computer became my vent. I realized how much hatred I harbored in my soul. By writing how I felt, I was able to pour it out of my head and onto paper. It no longer had to be congested and hidden to gnaw in my brain. I wrote out as much as I could and in the end, my pain was condensed in forty-four pages.

There were many more chapters that I had to write, but the main anger and frustrations were in those 44-pages. It felt good to get it out. It felt as if I were screaming it all out loud from the top of the tallest mountain for all to hear.

Unfortunately, my peace would soon become my bio mom's new pain to bear. I debated so many times whether or not to share this information with her. I didn't want her to get the wrong message.

Before I handed her the manuscript, I prefaced it by saying:

"Mom, I want to share something with you about my life. Before I do, however, I want you to understand and believe that you did what you thought was in the best interest in my life. I understand what you did was very unselfish and the most loving thing a mom could do with the situation that you were facing. Despite everything you are about to read, I think I came out okay."

While she read it, she cried and later told me that she cried for days afterwards. It was exactly what I didn't want to happen, but it was inevitable. I kept reassuring her I was okay and that I loved her.

Mom hugged me a lot and said how guilty she felt. She never expected me to be abused. After all, the thought is that those parents who decide to adopt are supposed to be even more loving since they want to have the child. She was devastated to find out otherwise. I kept telling her that no matter what, I knew she made the best decision at the time and not to have any regrets. That's easier said than done.

DAVID PELZER'S' TRILOGY

A few months after I started to write, I came across a book called "A Child Called 'It.'" It was the #1 New York Times bestseller. When I started reading it, I couldn't put it down. There were so many similarities in both our childhood and adult lives. There was someone else out there who experienced the same things I did, and worse. I was stunned by the contents of the book. His mom, too, had many of the same qualities that mine did; alcohol being one of them. Like mine, she blamed him for things he didn't do and would beat him.

In one incident, he tells of when his mother tried to burn him on the stove. When I read that, I realized how much of my memories were suppressed.

At that moment, I clearly remember when my adoptive mom told me to put out my hand. I was about eight-years-old. She had a cigarette in her hand and told me she'd beat me if I moved my hand. She came within a millimeter and I pulled away. I was then beaten. This wasn't one of the worst incidents that happened to me, but I find it strange that my brain would suppress this recollection. Perhaps only a psychiatrist would/might know why.

David Pelzer has gone on to the *Oprah Winfrey Show*, *Larry King Show* and a host of other speaking engagements. He stands firm on his tenet of *I'm not about child abuse. I'm not here to blame my mother. We all have problems but nothing can conquer the human spirit.*

While I completely agree with him, I believe that the child abuse should be directly addressed. Not with philosophies of the strength of the human spirit, but by recognizing, preventing, and helping the victims and the victimizers that seek help.

A few years ago, David did a book signing at a local bookstore. I was eager to meet him and share my manuscript. More importantly, I wanted to hear his story first hand and how he deals with the events in his childhood as an adult. I expected to hear some somber insight and was hoping to hear him give advice to adults and children in how to recognize and help those in need.

Instead, in an Arnold Schwarzenegger impression, he talked mostly about his life ambition to be a comedian. It wasn't what I expected and frankly, I was disappointed. I felt this was his opportunity to help others understand what we've been through. In its place, I heard a self-promoting, aggrandizing, comedian rather than a child abuse prevention advocate.

Perhaps, he felt his book had already put that message out and this was a chance to digress in a humorous way. I guess in my humble opinion, when given the opportunity to teach others how to prevent child abuse, that opportunity should be taken. I'm not against using humor in presentations. I do sprinkle humor into my own presentations in order to offset those parts of my story than tend to be uncomfortable for some. With all due respect to David, perhaps it was his way to not relive those past feelings and use this venue for his own happiness.

MOM'S MONTEREY VISIT: JOURNAL ENTRY
1/17/99, 10:06 PM (journal entry)
I have never felt this complete and at peace with my life than this weekend. My birth mom is sitting next to me watching TV. She keeps

telling me she is sorry for what I've gone through and I keep reassuring her that everything is okay and it was not her fault.

For me there is no touch that can equal the touch of my biological mother's hand. It is comforting, reassuring, loving, tender, and real. She holds my arm and my hand while squeezing them every so often. When she hugs me, the hugs last a little longer and are a little tighter than hugs I've received from others. For me, it is a birth mom hug. I've never known what I have missed until now.

Now and then she will bring me closer to plant a kiss on my cheek. I tell her I love her and she reciprocates the words. The inflection in her voice is not one that is merely an auto response that many of us have become so accustomed to. She says it softly, and with heartfelt conviction. She says it only the way a mother could say it to her son. She hugs, kisses, touches, and talks to me like I always dreamed she would. I cherish her and I cherish these moments. I don't want her to let go.

Me, Mom, and Mookie (my Chow Chow)

PUBLIC SPEAKER – CPS ASILOMAR RETREAT

In November of 2001, I was asked to deliver a presentation on my adoption/abuse experience at an annual retreat for Child Protection Services at the *Asilomar Conference Center* in Pacific Grove, CA. I was honored and petrified at the same time. As much as I loved public speaking, talking about something that was personal to a large venue was scary. The audience consisted of directors and social workers. Although I was used to sharing my story to social workers in a small classroom environment, this was different. In class, I wasn't the focal point. It was just a story to use as filler between course lessons. Students could choose to listen or not.

To add to my fear, I was the last speaker on a three-day venue. The attendees could have opted to leave since many of them had come from all corners of California to attend. This was a different stage; those who chose to stay actually stayed to hear what I had to say. Given the option to leave and get home early versus listening to me for forty-five minutes. I thought it would turn out to be a small audience. That wasn't the case.

There were easily over a hundred social workers in the room and my heart was in my throat. Once again, like the night I recited that Christmas poem, I found myself center stage. Those same butterflies in my stomach returned, except now they were bigger.

I began by saying, "My name is Claudio Antonio Ladron de Guevara Jr. The sad part of my name is not how long it is or how difficult it is to pronounce. It's the fact that the only things I know how to say in Spanish are *baño* and *cerveza*."

The audience laughed.

"I feel like the prodigal son after returning home from a very long journey. I started this journey with Monterey County CPS about six years ago when I was hired to teach CWS/CMS[13]. After a brief stint, I was contracted by IBM. I lived only a few blocks from here, so you can understand why I feel like this a homecoming event. I am currently contracted

---

13 Child Welfare System/Case Management System is a statewide database that Child Protection Services utilize to input and track child abuse cases.

with IBM as a consultant and trainer for CWS/CMS and have been residing in Sacramento for the last three years."

"If it were not for my social worker, I am sure I would not be here speaking to you today. In 1964, a social worker was assigned to my adoption case. I was a multi-ethnic newborn, which during that time period did not have a high market value. Caucasian babies were what the market was demanding. I was like a dot-com company in a potential portfolio of blue chip stocks."

"Six months later, fortunately for my social worker, a couple surfaced that was looking for diversity. It was most likely because they, too, were as diverse as I. My adoptive parents were first generation Japanese and Mexican. Perfect! The downside; this child will have to learn to eat sushi burritos and put wasabi on tacos. The alternative may have been long term foster care in a group home."

"Based on pictures, 8mm film and what little I have in term of memories, it seemed that I had a pretty happy early childhood. That, however, came to sudden halt at the age of five."

From there I shared what I could within my allotted time. There were many questions at the end asking how I dealt with it then and how I deal with it now. They were really interested in the long-term impact of being an abused child. They were looking for insight and the effect that it had on my adult life.

My time allotment exceeded the forty five minutes, but no one stopped me. In fact, they wanted to hear more.

At the conclusion of that presentation, I was emotionally and physically drained. I found myself, however, getting another surge of energy when I was approached by a handful of social workers that stood in a line, who came to thank or hug me.

One of the audience members asked "How can you tell a story like yours with humor?"

I responded with an incident that took place the previous summer when my brother Tommy took me out on Lake Oroville to teach me to kayak. He kept emphasizing to not dig my paddle in too deep on a turn or I'd capsize.

But as sure as night follows day; that's exactly what I did. I capsized in a river kayak tethered in by rubber skirting and could not get out. For what must have only been a minute (but felt like an eternity) of flailing about, I temporarily resigned myself to my situation and almost gave up. Geeze, I thought; my crummy headstone epitaph would read - Knucklehead brother drowns in Lake Oroville for not following instructions.

After spending seventeen years living in a physically and emotionally abusive situation and then another ten years in the military, what a quirk of fate it would be to see it come to an end like this. The irony was just a bit much for me to digest. With what little oxygen and strength I had left, I bent forward, found the neoprene skirt that had me trapped and pulled as hard as I possibly could.

I immediately popped out and when I reached the surface, all I could do was laugh hysterically. Not from hysteria, but at the thought of surviving and living another day.

I learned many lessons from that incident and I share those with others. It is the same for how I feel about what I experienced as a child. I survived and I learned from it. Having a sense of humor can help make it through many rough situations, but it also helps me to get through my stories a little easier. Now I can share my experience with others that, hopefully may benefit from it.

One lady thanked me for sharing my story. She said her story was similar but she was never able to share it with others. She now felt compelled to share her story so that others, too, would understand and help prevent another child from having to experience what we had experienced.

Another lady told me that I was an inspiration for her. She could now appreciate the thankless job that she does every day.

I told her that although she may not get a direct *thank you*, it will come indirectly many times over. When the children she helps grow up, they will be without the scars that she helped heal or prevent.

Others stepped up and asked me if they could just give me a hug, which I gladly accepted. I felt some of those hugs were meant for me, while others were for them. It was an awesome feeling.

9

An Unexpected Visit

F AST FORWARD TO 2005, I received a phone call from Victor, a neighbor friend who I had met after I bought my first home in Sacramento. Later I had bought another home not far from that neighborhood and was renting out the first home. It was late in the afternoon, and I hadn't heard from Victor in a few months. I was surprised to hear from him.

"Hey Tony, your parents are here."

I thought that it was weird that my newly found parents were over at Victor's house. They had helped me move to my new house and knew where I lived. Why would they be at the rental property address? I told Victor that they knew where I lived and to send them over.

"No man, you don't understand. Your other parents are here."

"What? You mean my adoptive parents? What the hell are they doing over there?" I couldn't believe what I was hearing.

"They came to find you and they had your old address. No one was home and they were asking the neighbors about you and they were directed to me for your new address."

I asked Victor to put my dad on the phone.

"Dad, what in the hell are you doing over there?"

He explained that he and my mom had hired a private investigator to find me and this was the address given to them. When I asked them why they were there, he responded that they wanted to know why I had chosen not to communicate with them. I told him that talking about it over the phone was not appropriate and they should come over.

When Victor got back on the phone, I told him that I'd be there to escort them back. He already knew that I didn't have the best relationship with them and he told me that he'd have them follow him over to my house. He knew I was stressing and needed time to compose myself.

When I told my wife that they were coming over, I could tell she was nervous. Rosa had never met them before and she had no time to prepare the house for the visit. She scrambled to get things in order, but since she kept the house meticulous I told her not to worry about it. It didn't help.

Then, I started pacing up-and-down the stairs. I couldn't think straight.

Why would they drive all the way from L.A. to come see me? I started to feel like a little kid again. I hated this feeling of the power they seemed to have over me. Why couldn't I feel like a full grown adult around them? When I heard the cars outside, I told myself *I have to be strong and man up to the situation.* I would just lay it out there as to how I felt then-and-now and the reason for not communicating with them.

I opened the door and watched my mom walk up the walkway. She looked old and couldn't walk without a forced and slow gait. She never got her full mobility back from the stroke. Dad was still in front of the car talking to Victor when I invited my mom to come in.

When she looked around, she was in awe of the home. It was a tri-level home with a large canvassed 8'X10' painting in the reception room.

I was enamored with the beautiful islands of Greece so the painting appeared as if you were looking out of your own backyard from a hill that overlooked the Aegean Sea.

Then there was a granite slab trough waterfall that was at the top of the first flight of steps leading to the huge kitchen. The floors were completely tiled in Italian gold flaked marble and in a customized diamond pattern.

As she looked around the house, she said, as if to herself, "I knew you would be successful one day."

What? Did my ears deceive me? Did I just hear what I thought she said? When did she know this? She never told me! In fact, she would always tell me that I'd amount to nothing; a ditch digger, a loser, an unsuccessful nobody.

Those putdowns and cutting remarks were hammered into my head almost daily as far back as I could remember.

Now she had the audacity to say that she *always knew*? Why the hell didn't she tell me then?

In spite of my success, I've never felt successful. I thought I still hadn't measured up. Even this house didn't feel like a sign of success for me until this point. *Damn her again!*

I didn't respond to what she said. When my dad came up the walkway, I watched. He, too, looked older than what I expected. It was sobering to see how much my dad had aged since I last saw him. He looked frail. He no longer had those massive arms that I could remember or his physically intimidating stature.

When he walked in, he too, looked around the house. "Your house is beautiful."

I escorted them up the short flight of stairs that lead into the kitchen. It was also done with Italian marble and granite slabs throughout.

My mom just kept looking as if she couldn't believe her eyes. She kept saying how nice the house was.

As dad sat down on the leather couch, my dad said, "It looks like you are doing well for yourself."

I sat down next to them and Rosa came into the room to introduce herself.

I could only imagine how she was feeling at this point. She knew everything about them and I knew she was nervous too.

My parents were cordial and said they were *pleased to meet her.* She gave them the obligatory smile and from there, excused herself to the kitchen to get drinks and some hors d'oeuvres.

"So why did you drive all the way up here from Carson?"

"We wanted to know *Why?* Why did you just stop communicating with us? We haven't heard from you in four years!"

I told them that I wasn't happy with being accused of stealing from my mom, or how she addressed my wife in the voicemail.

Of course my mom responds with, "I never accused you of stealing and I never called your wife a bitch!"

I wasn't going to counter her response, because it would have been a no-win situation.

I went on to tell them I never felt I measured up to their expectations and didn't feel like they raised me properly with all the beatings I got from Mom.

My dad jumped in with, "Your Mom never beat you. She raised you the best way she thought possible. She loves you like you were her own son! She's your mother and you shouldn't treat her like that!"

"Dad, you weren't there for all the times she hit me. Do you remember when she hit me with the military police baton?"

"I never hit you with that!" she interjected.

I was in the twilight zone. Everything I brought up was quashed or denied. It was as if I was living in Bizarro World[14] while I was growing up and then transplanted to Reality World as an adult.

This conversation wasn't going the way I had planned. It didn't matter what I'd say, it was denied. I felt as if I were chasing my own tail. They were just completely convinced that they did nothing wrong.

After all, look around this house. This was a testimonial to them as great parents!

No! This was all in spite of them, not because of them! They didn't get that! I didn't push the conversation. My point was not going to be made today and probably not ever. There was no talking to them about how I felt. It was simply pointless.

---

14 In Superman Comics Bizarro and the Bizarro World have become somewhat well known in popular culture, and the term Bizarro is used as to describe anything that utilizes twisted logic or that is the opposite of something else.

The conversation ran its course and we were at an impasse. Dad said mom was tired and they were renting a hotel nearby.

I'm glad they did, because having them there any longer would have been uncomfortable and awkward.

When they left, I felt as though I had taken ten steps backwards.

ANOTHER CONFRONTATION

After mom and dad's unexpected visit, Mom would call me whenever she felt the need. She would complain about her relationship with Dad and how she wasn't happy. While this situation defined their relationship as far back as I could remember, this time it was exacerbated by a contractor who ripped them off in a remodeling scam.

Mom was always big on paying for things in cash. She felt it was a way to leverage for a better deal. Also, not being familiar with the law and her rights, she was conned into giving the contractor half of the money upfront, which was about $5,000.00.

In the end, the contractor ripped them off by not completing the work. Needless to say she was livid. As a result, she found fault with my dad and was unrelenting in her berating of him for not pursuing the matter as she saw fit. So she turned to me for help.

I researched the contractor's license number and found that he didn't have one. I made phone calls to the *Better Business Bureau* and tried to seek some legal recourse for her.

The contractor covered his tracks well and I wasn't able to find much in the way of a real name or address. He most likely used an alias and temporary cell phone number.

Mom called me every day at all times of the day wanting to see what I could find or do. She was angered that I wouldn't immediately pick up the phone or return her calls.

I told her that unless the contractor could physically be found; there wasn't much she could do. I also tried to explain to her that I had a life of my own and couldn't just drop everything in my life to be at her beck-and-call. With that she said, "Then you aren't worth a good goddamn!"

My immediate response, "What the fuck did you say to me? You might be able to talk to Dad like that, but you won't talk to me like that! Who in the hell do you think you are? I'm not a little child anymore and you will never talk to me like that again! Do you hear and understand that?"

I threw my cell phone across the room. While it felt good to say that, it wasn't enough. I wanted to go through that phone line and strangle her. I couldn't believe she still talked to me like that! I was so angry.

This was the end for me. I never wanted to hear her voice again.

Despite it being in pieces on the other side of the room, my cell phone kept ringing incessantly.

When I calmed down, I managed to partially put the phone back together and listened to the voicemails. It was my dad reminding me that she was still my mom and I shouldn't disrespect her.

Did he lose his mind?

I don't care who a person is, they will get the same respect that is given to me. I wanted to call him and tell him that he and I shared different views on respect. I knew that it would only fall on deaf ears. He would defend her to the end. Realizing this, I stomped the phone into tiny plastic and metal pieces which turned out to be an expensive, but well worth it *symbolic tantrum.*

It was just a matter of months before, yet, another confrontation took place.

I'm sure my mom drove my dad to the brink of insanity on a daily basis for allowing me to talk to her in the manner I'd spoken to her. I felt sorry for him.

To this day, I can't understand how one person allows another to have that much power or influence over them. I guess it goes back to how we were raised and what we accepted as *normal.*

Six months later, there was a loud knock on my door. It was them again.

This time I stood in the doorway without inviting them in. "What the hell are you doing here?" I asked in shock.

"Your mother wants to know what your problem is!" my dad yelled at me.

"Are you kidding me? You drove all the way out here to find out what my problem is? Do you not recall all the abuse Mom put me through?"

"I never abused you!" She shot back.

This was the *Twilight Zone Part II*. There were the two people I called *Mom* and *Dad* that abused me as a child, standing on the front door steps of my house yelling at me!

This was a Saturday afternoon and the neighbors were out.

Was this really happening? Better yet, why was I allowing this to happen?

I felt a resurgence of power coming from within my soul. "Get the fuck off my property! You are not welcomed here and you are trespassing! Get the fuck off my property NOW! I own this house and the property it sits on. Get the fuck out of here!"

I slammed the door in their face, dead bolted the door, then turned around and sat on the steps leading up to the kitchen.

It took every ounce of physical and emotional strength to do and say what I did. I felt drained, but somewhat vindicated.

That was eight years ago; I have not seen them since.

ANOTHER GIFT

While I have not physically seen my parents in over eight years, they still attempted to communicate with me.

On one occasion, I received a pickup notice from UPS. They had sent a package to me. Although I was curious as to the contents, I didn't want whatever it was (I wondered if it was another deflated basketball?).

As far back as I can remember, Mom always told me to never ask them for anything after I left the house. Those words became tattooed on my brain. I would always respond back to her *not to worry*; I wouldn't ask her for anything, even if it meant saving me from an agonizing death.

That said; there have been a few situations in the past where I could have used their help financially. But, I would have rather stabbed myself in the eye than ask for it.

After several attempts by UPS to have the gift delivered, it was eventually sent back to the sender.

When they received it back, Mom was livid and she made sure my cell phone voicemail was filled with expletives telling me so. It was pretty clear she wasn't happy about having her gift returned. She said it was something I always wanted.

Sorry, but apologies and validation cannot be packaged.

The reason for not accepting the gift is deeper than not wanting anything from her. It's as if whatever this gift was, my acceptance of it would absolve her of all that she had put me through. Given that it was so important to her to give it to me, I felt as though I had some power over her.

She now knew how it felt to want something but not ever being able to get it. In this case it would be absolution.

I have to digress for a minute and explain the emotional impact of receiving letters from them. You see, it's almost as if they were right in front of me and I find myself regressing back to a five-year-old. When words are delivered verbally, there is impact. When words are delivered in written form, they have an even bigger impact.

When the letters are from my dad on behalf of my mom, the impact is like an emotional atomic bomb. Due to this, my wife always opens the letters first and gives me the watered down *Cliff Notes* summary. Even then, it's not enough to diffuse the explosion.

I received one of the letters in the summer of 2007 in response to some roses that I had sent to my mom for *Mother's Day*.

I was having a sentimental moment. I didn't expect that the delivery service would give them my new home address in Lincoln, CA which my adoptive parents didn't have.

The letter stated that Mom had wanted to personally thank me for the roses and give me the gift she tried to send to me months before. They had made it all the way to the town I lived in (I'd moved again), and they couldn't find my actual address. They ended up driving all the way back to Los Angeles.

I thought to myself, *why didn't they just go to the local post office or police station?*

The thing that bothered me the most is, despite their last disastrous visit, they felt they could just show up at my front door unannounced.

Of several letters sent to me, somehow the following letter didn't find its way to the trash can. Unlike the rest, there were no expletives or accusations. This time it was a letter trying to impose guilt:

October 30, 2007

Tony,

This one might come as a surprise to you, but here I am writing to you a short letter. We hope you and your wife will be enjoying good health. As for us, we're not too good, not too bad, just here.

Ok, the reason I am writing to you now is because we know that you moved to this new address and I looked in the map and the only thing I know is that this place is north of Sacramento. Part of the reason to know where your new place is because your mom wants to see you and give you a present she got for you sometime back. If you want to tell me how to get to your new place, I would really be happy to know how to get there. If you'd much rather meet us someplace else where we can get there and you can get there with no problem from your place also, just let us know ASAP. If this arrangement fits better with what your plans are, let me know. Or maybe you don't want to see us anymore, I don't know. We sure would be happy to see you once more or maybe a whole bunch of times before the man upstairs decides that we spent enough time on this earth. I want you to call me or mama.

Hoping to Hear from You Soon
Mom & Dad

I had never responded to any of their letters, and I wasn't about to start now. It would only fuel the fire with the things I truly wanted to write. In the end, their denial of what they did to me would only frustrate me.

THE IMPACT

"The strongest swords of steel have been forged through the hottest furnace fires," is a saying that was shared with me by cousin Jory and is a reflection of my life. I am a stronger person because of this. I would not wish, however, that anyone find their strength through tribulations such as this. Strength should be gained from support of loved ones, not hate or abuse.

I am driven; driven to perfection and achievement. Is this good? No, not for me; I don't view these virtues as positive attributes. It is an ever-consuming drive for validation, recognition, perfection and acceptance. All those things that I didn't get as a child are those things that drive me now.

Yes, I do get those things now from friends, colleagues and other sources, but those are not the ones that mean the most to me. If only I could hear the words: "I am proud of you. You did good..." from my adoptive mother's lips, I probably would feel my achievements were something of which I could be proud. It would be ideal if it was punctuated at the end with "I'm sorry for telling you I hated you, never wanted you, and for spitting on you."

I don't believe my abuse was extreme compared to thousands of other cases that are out there. I've read many stories much more horrific than my case, including David Pelzer's story. It doesn't make the hurt any less painful. While physical pain can be measured on a scale of 1-10, emotional pain doesn't have a range scale. It goes deep and it can last a lifetime. Words cut deeper than knives and hit harder than bats or belts. While physical scars heal and in most cases disappear, emotional trauma can be an infection and lead to worse situations, including passing it on to the next generations. This cycle of abuse is vicious and those who are part of it need to know how to break it.

Far be it that I was perfect. I had my moments of childhood mischief and adolescent rebellion. Even so, it was unexceptional. Looking back to who I was, I see an innocent child. One that never deserved any of the treatment he was subjected to. This was someone who would do just about anything to receive praise and validation. I see a youth that just wanted to be loved; only to be stripped of an innocence that only a young child could experience. The determination to be the best at whatever he attempted was only met with chastisement and indignity.

On my right arm and shoulder, I have a tribal tattoo of a fire breathing dragon. Within the dragon in Chinese characters, an inscription reads, "Achieving Success." The dragon represents my Chinese zodiac sign. The main symbolism, however, is what the dragon represents to me.

When I was a teenager my mom told me that she would disown me if I ever got a tattoo. It took four and half hours of incredible pain. When it was done, I felt a release; a severed connection that was long overdue.

LOOKING IN FROM OUTSIDE

The toughest part of my life now is watching my friends as they attempt to raise their own children. Not too long ago, my wife and I decided to have breakfast with our neighbors and their children. The husband, a big and stocky police officer, and his wife, have three children. The little girl, eight-years-old, and boy, five-years-old, are from her previous marriage. Their newborn arrived shortly after their recent marriage.

One morning we all decided to go to the local pancake house for breakfast. As one would expect a five-year-old to act, he was fidgety and bored. But unlike other five-year-old kids I've seen getting out of hand, this one was just inquisitive about when his food was coming. Otherwise he just colored and wanted validation for his artwork.

Jack, (not his real name), got directly into his son's face and pretty much told him to shut his mouth or suffer the consequences.

The fear and confusion that the five-year-old showed on his face was one I knew all too well. My heart dropped and I felt helpless. I knew it wasn't my place to say anything to Jack. He got even more miffed when the baby started to cry.

He made it loud and clear he hated when babies cried in public and his own was no exception.

I had to momentarily step outside to maintain my composure. I was torn in taking a stance and losing a friendship or keeping to myself and letting the chips fall where they may.

Jack's eight-year-old stepdaughter will be most affected.

I watched Jack during Christmas day (when we were invited over for dinner). I don't know what the situation was, but I watched him take his stepdaughter into a hallway and yell in her face to make his point. She was terrified and in tears. Fortunately, the grandmother was there to witness the event and interceded on behalf of the little girl.

The mother knew full well what was going on and did nothing. The argument between grandmother and the stepfather escalated in full public view and it was very uncomfortable for me to witness. It was, however, a good feeling to see another adult step in to tell this man his child rearing approach was out of line.

From that point on, I pretty much ostracized them from our lives. They don't know why we no longer talk to them and I feel like a coward for not telling them. If I did, I knew that I'd be told to *mind your own business* and/or **you don't have children of your own, so don't assume to know how to raise ours.** It's the *damned if I do, damned if I don't* syndrome.

In the end, I suspect many people find themselves in this very situation. If so, do as I will, bookmark this page and leave a copy on their doorstep anonymously. Perhaps we can make a difference in a child's life with this gesture.

Watching friends raise their children badly is difficult, but watching other parents in public is just as bad. Here's one that affected me deeply.

RAISING CHILDREN BADLY

September 17, 1999: Journal Entry

Today I witnessed an incident that will not be forgotten. It was as if someone decided to take an old butter knife and attempted to etch out an intricate design onto a crystal vase; that vase being my memory. As I stood in line of a fast food restaurant, I watched a mother berate her son for not being able to quickly decide what he wanted. He couldn't have been more than five years old. As the mother bent down into the boy's face to yell at him, he flinched to cover his face. When the mother didn't strike him, he reached out to hug her leg for consolation.

In that instant, I became that little boy. I felt what I thought he was feeling. At that same moment my heart sank and I wanted to cry.

I tried to disassociate myself from the event but I couldn't. I became angry with that mother. I wanted to tell her how much of a negative impact she was having on her child. I wanted to tell her when he grows up, there would be a good chance that he will resent her and the pain she inflicted today will come back to her later.

I wanted to humiliate this mother in front of everyone just as she did that little boy. I wanted to be a superhero for that little boy. But even if I dared to, he would only view me as an intrusive outsider. I would have become the mother's archrival, an enemy, a zero and not a hero. It looks like I'll be carrying a duffel bag filled with copies of this book and handing them out whenever I witness these situations.

As I internalize this, I realize that this imagined conflict I'm having with his mother is my own inner conflict. It is a confrontation that I wish I could have. The hero I want to be is the hero that I wish was there for me when I was five-years-old. It is years of pent up anger that I need to release. It is negative energy and it is wasted energy.

Objectively, all this is easy to acknowledge. What is difficult is to concede to therapy. Yes, I wrote *concede*, as to give in or forfeit.

Therapy; I struggled with this venture. Those who knew my story would usually ask me if thought about counseling or psychological therapy. My adoptive Mom always told me I *needed to see a shrink*, and that *there was something wrong with me*.

To me therapy denotes one's own admission that they are broken; that something is psychologically wrong and needs fixing. I don't want to admit I am broken. My mother was broken, not me. Why should I have to go to therapy? If anyone needs to go, it would be her, right? Sure I'm right. Like me; she doesn't think she is broken either.

Here is how I envisioned my initial therapy session:

"Good afternoon Mr. Guevara, why are you here?"...

"I want answers."

He or she is going to tell me he or she can't give me answers. That the answers have to come from me, and he or she can only guide me in the appropriate direction.

Then I will say, "Then how can you help me?" (He or she is going to tell me that he or she can't help me, and that he or she can only help me help myself.)

Then I'll ask, "How much is this going to cost me?" (He or she is going to reply with, *is it the money that you are concerned with, or your mental well-being*?).

Then the conversation and the therapy sessions will continue with me asking, "Do you people always answer questions with questions and give answers that are not definitive or concrete?"

With a response of, "The human mind is not definitive or concrete. Everyone thinks and behaves differently. Why do you ask this question?"

I'll say, "Oh no, you are not going to trick me into that one. I know what your next question is going to be. I'm one step ahead of you."

He or she will say, "So what is my next question?"

I'll respond, "That one, the one you just asked. That's the question! (Please help me; I'm in psychoanalysis hell!)."

The consensus will be, "I'm sorry, only you can help you...."

And so went my self-induced therapy nightmare. On top of all this, my other struggle was talking to a complete stranger about things that are extremely personal. This person doesn't actually care about me. More than likely, they haven't been through what I have been through. How can they relate to how and what I feel? My "guidance" is going to come from a college textbook.

So just for argument's sake, what if I do find a therapist I feel comfortable with? I can just see myself in what I perceive as a successful first session. There I am just spilling out my soul and then out of the blue in mid-sentence I hear, *I'm sorry Tony, but our hour is up. We'll have to continue this in our next session.*

And here is where I become a bona fide 5150 and would just completely lose it. Hell, for the time and money I would spend on this therapist, I could just send myself through school and fix myself! Once that's done, I can charge others and finally afford to buy a home in Monterey!

Yup, I am going to be a therapists' worst nightmare. I'll be lucky if anyone takes my case.

Postscript: I actually did find two therapists recently that were nowhere close to how I imagined them to be. They helped me to understand things about myself that I didn't understand before. These were real people with real feelings, not the cold robotrons I thought they would be. During my therapy sessions, they, too, had to reach for the *Kleenex* box to wipe away their own tears from listening to my story. One of them had adopted a baby girl who was now a teenager. My therapy sessions became her learning sessions in that she was now having the perspective of an adoptee child's viewpoint.

MY ADOPTIVE MOTHER'S MIND

My adoptive mother was raised in Japan during the latter part of World War II. She came from an extremely dysfunctional family that struggled to make it from hand to foot. With three brothers and two sisters, she was the second oldest in the family. She would tell me stories of how she was the school reject because she came from an impoverished family. She would be picked on and beaten by her schoolmates. Due to her responsibilities of taking care of her younger siblings, she was unable to complete her education. Basic survival and abuse by family and friends on a daily basis was the world she came to know.

My mother never hid the fact she was raped when she was a teenager. She talked about it openly and angrily. It was because of this tragic event that she was unable to have children of her own. What made it even more tragic was the rapist was her brother. I suspect he also victimized my aunt; the one that molested me.

As I matured, it is my belief that I became a symbolic manifestation of what her brother was to her. He was a player of women, a rebel, and a manipulator.

I had been dating several different girls at a time when I was in high school. I'm sure my lack of fidelity to those girls was a mark of disrespect of women to her. I represented all the reprehensible attributes that were like those of her brother's. Her hatred towards me and her reasons for wanting a daughter are quite clear here. It may also explain her manipulation of my earlier relationships as well.

She built up a great deal of hostility, anger, and hatred towards her family. I know she wanted badly to confront her own mother to tell her about the rape and other issues. She wanted to vent and she wanted closure. This was just around the time her parents passed away. I don't know if she was ever able to purge any of what she had gone through to her parents. I only wish that she had not waited so long. Maybe, just maybe, I wouldn't have been as abused as I was.

In dissecting the events in my mother's life from a psycho-sociological view, I've attempted to reason and understand her thinking processes. The human mind is extremely complex and I don't claim to be an expert in this arena. I can only speculate what went through her mind. In light of all the combining events in both her and my life, I am convinced that she loved me. As strange as this may seem, the way she loved me was only different in how others love their own children. Her method of expression was only based on the way it was shown to her. Perhaps in my attempt to understand the psychology from an objective viewpoint, I am attempting to forgive her actions.

From her stories about being tied to the rafters by her ankles and left to hang there for several hours, it is apparent that her own father and mother were abusive to her. This would justify in her mind that the punishments I received were warranted because they were only a fraction of what she had experienced. She would not understand that her behavior towards me would be construed as abusive.

In fact, to this day she would verifiably defend herself by stating that she did all the things she did to me out of love. She would tell anyone that the reason I turned out so well was due to her methods of raising me. Even if it were true, the consequence of her actions has caused her to lose her son.

My father still can't quite grasp my love/hate relationship for her. The one time I tried to tell him what she had done to me as a child was met with an instant defense.

"She's your mother. She's all you got. It's the past, let it go."

To this I responded with:

"No Dad, it's not the past. I live it every day. My wound has not healed and it remains an open sore. I want Mom to understand how I feel about what she has done to me. When she can truly understand and feel remorse for the pain she has caused me, only then will I allow the healing process to begin."

When I wrote the paragraph above, I had not yet realized how important it is to let the healing process begin as soon as possible. If not, the wound will grow and have a very negative impact on one's life. Life is much too short to harbor negative thoughts. *Like attracts like* is what I've learned over the recent months. If I do not forgive, I may not be forgiven. We control our thoughts and our feelings and not the other way around.

Whenever I see a young child, I see an innocence that I lost at the age of five. I see the shared love of a mother and child I never experienced. That was taken from me.

I am still living in the fear of getting hurt by those closest to me. As such, I trust few and I'm constantly on my guard. There are no more tears that I will cry as a result of something my mom will do to me. I no longer live in that world. My adoptive mom claims she loved me. If that was love, then I want no part of it.

In my opinion, parenting classes should be mandatory. I believe we learn our own parenting skills based on how we were raised. How we were raised obviously doesn't mean it was the best way. There is always room for improvement, if not completely different parenting methods altogether.

10

Bio Mom Reveals another Secret

S EVERAL MONTHS AFTER Mom and Marvin moved to California, we had another family get together at their house. As usual, the boys were in the guest room playing X-box when Mom rounded us up along with Lisa. She said she had something to tell us but wanted to tell us privately. We all wondered what it was and even joked about whether there was another secret sibling. We had no idea how accurate our joke was until she told us about another child by the name of Gwyn.

Mom told us that Gwyn had recently found out that our biological mom was her mother too, and that she'd discovered it by happenstance.

Apparently when Gwyn was preparing for her marriage, she needed her baptismal certificate. When she went to the church to get a copy, the name on the certificate had our biological mom's maiden name on it (after talking with Gwyn later, I discovered that was only partially true).

For me this was exciting news to know that I had another sister. Moreover, her adoption circumstances triggered even more questions; many more. I wanted to know how her family life was. Did she know she was adopted prior to the baptismal certificate discovery? If so, did she also deal with a cultural and/or identity crisis? Was she abused as I had been? Where did she grow up? Did she have brothers and sisters?

My mind, yet again, was going a million miles an hour.

I looked at the reactions of my siblings and could tell that Lisa and Tommy were surprised, but outwardly happy. James, always the stoic and more cynical of the group, replied to our mom in a tongue-in-cheek manner, "Any other kids you want to tell us about?"

We all laughed when Mom said, *"No, that's all."*

She went on to say Gwyn was excited to meet us. I asked her if Gwyn knew about my situation. Mom said it was my story to tell and would leave that up to me.

Mom did share with us that Gwyn was a semi-pro tennis player, living in Colorado and had four children. She went to *Mount Saint Mary's College* and grew up in Southern California with parents that were financially above average. Aside from that, I don't remember much of what she said.

I was caught up in my own thoughts, as well as when we could plan on our next bigger family reunion. That night I wrote an email to Gwyn to welcome her into her new sibling circle. She wrote back that she was looking forward to meeting us all in the near future. I didn't tell her about my situation since I wanted to share this with her in person.

Several months had gone by and when I asked Lisa about corresponding with Gwyn, she said there was a couple of generic courtesy emails that were exchanged, but beyond that not much more. I could tell Lisa was a little put off by this lack of correspondence. From there, the whole subject of Gwyn just waned and nothing more was said.

GWYN'S STORY

Fast forward another five years. As I was finalizing the manuscript to this book, I realized that there's a big missing puzzle piece to this story. I couldn't just finish this book without knowing what happened to Gwyn. How did her adopted life compare to mine? What were the differences in our emotional, physical, and psychological environments?

The list of questions in my head only grew. With this, I decided to take action by sending her a draft manuscript to this book. This was her response:

My dearest brother,

I cannot tell you how deeply and profoundly touched I am that you contacted me. Your manuscript has completely rocked me and all I know is that I feel an overwhelming need to meet you and very soon.

Several years ago, I tiptoed into the idea of getting to know you and our mother and brothers and sister. I think I felt so much fear that I just backed off. I can't explain it.

I need that connection to my blood relatives. It's an inexplicable need that only you and I can understand. Your writing has unearthed feelings that I have tried to bury for 40 years now. I feel a sense of relief and a sense of urgency at the same time to fill that "hole in the soul."

Again, I would very much like to meet in person, is there a way we can arrange something like that?

Much love,

Your sister,

Gwyn

Hey sis,

I kept looking at my Blackberry since I sent that email out last night. The anticipation was overbearing and I am so glad you've expressed your desire to connect!! I spoke with Mom last night about my intention and we both agreed that having a reunion soon for all of us would be phenomenal! I will speak with Mom and start looking at possible dates. She had mentioned something in the summer but I'm thinking about something closer to Mother's Day for all of us. Typically this would be the day that we'd all converge to Mom's house. What do you think?

I, however, would love to meet you in person sooner! Given our adoption circumstances, I think our bond will be different. I've so much to share with you and so many questions to ask. I'm not sure how the logistics would work out but we'll see how our schedules look, yes? At the very least, let's talk on the phone!!! I can't wait to hear from you!

Please call when you can. I've attached pictures of my family.

Hey brother -

I didn't check my email until this morning; otherwise, I would have answered right away!

I love the idea of Mother's Day. Actually, my birthday is May 8, which is the day before Mother's Day and I can't think of a better gift than reuniting with all of you!

I'm so eager to talk with you! You are in California, right? Whereabouts? When would be a good time for you to talk? I'm an hour ahead of you in Denver.

I loved the pictures of all of you. I kept looking at you and my nephew (I love saying that!) looking for resemblances. I know you know what it's like. I'm attaching pics of me and my bunch! My husband is Mike, then the kids are Taylor (she will be 20 next week), Courtney (18), Alec (my 15 year old stepson), Jackson (10) and Lauren (8). Never a dull moment.

Let me know when you can talk on the phone :) I can't wait!

Lots of love,

Your sister

After these emails, we agreed to talk on the phone.

I found myself writing down questions as I did prior to Mom's first phone call 10 years earlier. Again, the anticipation was overwhelming, but this time it was different. There was no fear of rejection or a possible negative outcome. It was like having a huge jigsaw puzzle that had been assembled for years, but one piece was lost. Even though one could clearly see what the puzzle was, the missing piece stood out and took away from the beauty of an otherwise fully assembled and complicated art piece.

An hour prior to the phone call, I sat down pen and pad in hand with all my written questions. If I didn't, I knew I'd get caught up in the moment and forget a bunch of things I wanted to ask her.

After we talked, we immediately started to make plans on when we'd see each other. I thought what day would be better than *Mother's Day*? Because it was months away, it would give us plenty of time to coordinate a big family reunion and give Tommy, who was living in Alaska, enough time to fit it into his busy schedule.

Needless to say, when Mom found out, she was overjoyed at the prospect of having all her kids under her roof for the first time.

As the planning commenced, the reunion would include Courtney; Gwyn's daughter who was attending *San Francisco State University* as well as Delia, her adoptive mom. I knew from my own experience that the emotional build up to this event would increase exponentially as the time drew nearer. I knew what Gwyn would be feeling the day she arrived.

GWYN ARRIVES

Tommy arrived a day earlier than Gwyn to help get the house prepared for Gwyn's arrival and moreover, to just catch up after a year and half of not seeing each other. Tommy didn't know Gwyn's story so I took it upon myself to share some of it, especially the part about why she chose not to meet us sooner. I explained to him that it was the same feeling I had when I had met him and my other siblings for the first time. I wanted to be the older successful brother that was going to help in any way possible. I wanted to show them that I was there to add to the family and not take anything away. It was important for me to present myself as successful and one that could be looked up to. I knew that Gwyn would feel similarly.

The day that Gwyn was to arrive, Tommy, Rosa and I sat around the kitchen table discussing what we could do to make Gwyn's arrival a memorable and fun one. It was decided that Tommy and I would dress up in mascot suits that I owned from my mascot company. Tommy dressed up as an oversized comical dragon and I would be Scooby Doo. Rosa brought out her portable speakers and iPod on which she'd play *Who Let the Dogs Out*? Tommy and I would then come out from the side of the house where we were hiding and dance our way down the driveway.

When Marvin pulled up in the car with Gwyn and Delia, on cue, Tommy and I danced our way down the driveway. Since there's only a small area from where one can see out of the costume, we were pretty much dancing blindly and into each other.

It must have been a sight to see because I could hear my sister laughing hysterically. It was the reaction I wanted as I knew it would take some of the stress off Gwyn's shoulders.

She came up to us without knowing who was who and hugged us. It was a wonderful way to start our reunion.

Me, Gwyn, and Tommy

When I took off the head portion of the outfit, we both looked at each other like the first time I looked at Tommy. It was the look of seeing someone for the first time that had similar physical features as your own. The first thing I noticed was her eyes; they were the same light brown as mine and slightly almond shaped. It was one of the first things I noticed on Tommy when I saw him for the first time. Her eyes sparkled and smiled back and there was no denying just how happy she was to see me. Her tight hug was the icing on the cake. She and Tommy hugged immediately after and the same observations between them took place.

I walked over to Delia, Gwyn's adoptive mom, and gave her a big hug. She was beside herself in laughter and I could tell she was extremely happy for Gwyn and the reunion that was taking place before her eyes. Our mom and Marvin were in hysterics as well, but they were not surprised as they knew all too well, my humorous side.

As we all came into the house and congregated into the kitchen, I found myself stealing short glimpses of my sister. I was fascinated to see how her facial features were similar to my own. I thought I caught her doing the same and I smiled to myself knowingly. The excitement and the energy levels were intoxicating. It was an indescribable high.

As the day went on, Gwyn seemed to find her place. I felt her trepidation and her nervousness slowly slip away, but I could tell her walls were still slightly up. I knew too well how her mind was processing all this information. It must have been as overwhelming as it had been for me, when I met my family for the first time. It felt as though time was in a vacuum and your whole life came down to this very moment in time. Every hour seems to pass in a second and one wishes it would all just slow down.

The following day we had some alone time to talk. I could tell she had a lot on her mind and she wanted to get it out. As I had thought from my own experience, she was scared that Tommy, Lisa, and James would not accept her with open arms. Her fear with Tommy was allayed, but there was still Lisa and James to meet. I knew she was especially nervous meeting Lisa as Lisa would no longer be the only girl in the family. I remember feeling that way about James since he would no longer be regarded as the older brother. I told her not to worry about such things because all that mattered was that we are all one again. However, words often cannot trump overwhelming emotion.

Gwyn went on to share personal things about her life that are not in my right to share in this book. I can say, however, that we shared many issues common to adoptees. The main issue is not knowing who we are or where we come from.

Unlike me, Gwyn was adopted by Mom's 2nd cousin (and contrary to the original baptism certificate story), Gwyn had actually found out that she was adopted by mistake when overhearing a conversation that her cousin was adopted. When Gwyn asked whether, in fact, her cousin was adopted, she was told, "Yes, and so were you."

She was seven-years-old at the time, and she said she had a hard time processing this information. She added she was also told that Auntie Virgie was not her aunt, but was her actual birth mother. When she told me how this information was presented to her, my jaw dropped. Gwyn was asked to not tell Auntie Virgie that she knew the truth and this made for an awkward situation whenever Mom would visit with Gwyn and her family.

To this day, I can still recall the finer details of exactly how my adoption was presented to me. This was in stark contrast to how this information was given to Gwyn. My heart hurt for her as she shared this with me.

I asked Gwyn how she felt about the manner in which the information about her birth was presented, and she said *it really did not matter*. She said *the outcome was the same* and she *felt like an outsider*. She *felt disconnected* as if she *were no longer part of the family*.

As she said this, I relived that very moment in time when I had the exact same feeling. It was surreal and a feeling that no five-year-old could articulate. A seven-year-old could not do any better. It was all a bundle of negative emotions and I related to her feelings spot on.

There really is no way to convey to a non-adoptee the feeling of not belonging; of not having a blood connection. It feels as though you are on a small island crowded with people and yet, you still feel alone. I can't explain it any better way.

She shared with me a time when our mom came around to visit. She said she felt awkward because mom didn't know Gwyn knew the truth. We talked for about two hours and after lots of tears and Kleenexes, I could see a large weight had lifted from her shoulders. She gave me a big hug and thanked me for bringing us all together. I thanked her back for allowing it.

Later that day we headed to the train station to pick up her daughter, Courtney. After hugging her mom, she gave me just as big of a hug. The first thing she said was that she knew immediately that I was her mom's brother because of the resemblance. Gwyn later told me how neat it felt to have Courtney tell her that. It was a first of many firsts to come for Gwyn.

The next day was Gwyn's birthday. I woke up early to pick up some flowers, balloons, and pastries for her from all of us. When she awakened, she was pleasantly surprised at all her birthday loot and gave all of us big, tight, warm hugs. Her eyes sparkled with happiness and contentment. As simple as it was in presentation, I knew it would be a birthday and a weekend that she would never forget.

Later that morning we headed to Mom's for our family reunion. This was what I thought to be the pinnacle to Gwyn's emotional journey. And while I did what I could to comfort her, I knew she was probably even more nervous about this get-together than the one we had that morning. All those feelings of not wanting to impose on someone else's relationship had to have been resurfacing. (She later told me that meeting Tommy and me first had made her that much more comfortable with this situation).

As we walked to the door, we were greeted by both Delia and our mom. Lisa and Gwyn hugged each other. It was not the same hug that Lisa gave me when we first met. I felt awkward for Gwyn as I knew how important that moment was.

Immediately after, Gwyn bent down[15] and gave James a hug and he returned it as best he could. James is not the physical hugging type. It was what I had expected (it was good).

I tried not to appear too focused on the new interactions, but my heart was right there with Gwyn's as I tried to get a read on her. She seemed to be doing okay and I kept her in my peripheral; feeling very protective of her.

Eventually, Lisa and Gwyn sat at the dining table and were engaged in conversation. From where I stood, it seemed more cordial than a heartfelt sister/sister reunion.

In time, however, Lisa found herself sequestered in a spare bedroom citing her need to study for college finals. For me, this action would have been devastating, but perhaps I am more emotional about these things than others. I spoke to Gwyn afterwards and she said she felt Lisa was distant.

When I asked Lisa how she felt, she stated she was overwhelmed with the situation. She went on to say Tommy and I were much more extroverted and already had bonding time with Gwyn and she felt intimidated.

Years have passed since that first meeting. Gwyn and Lisa have since formed a great relationship and are now closer than ever.

That night Mom and Dad put together an awesome feast for all of us. It was just like the day I met the family for the first time. There was and always is enough food to feed a small army unit, but that is also a part of our Filipino culture. If you leave the house hungry, then it was your fault, not the host's fault.

After birthday cake, ice cream, and more food, we had to pick ourselves up and head back to my house since Mom & Marvin ran out of room for all of us to stay there for the night.

I tried to get a pulse read on Gwyn. It appeared all was okay and it seemed the final weight of this reunion lifted.

---

15 James suffered a spinal cord injury in a surfing accident in 2000, and is quadriplegic. He was in a wheelchair when Gwyn leaned down to kiss him.

When we got back to my house, we all settled down in the living room to watch TV. Somehow we ended up watching *The Notebook*, and found ourselves sniffling and blubbering at the end of the movie. While others may find this trivial, even funny, it was just another one of those family firsts; not just for Gwyn but for all of us. Somehow I felt it was just another milestone of bringing us that much closer together.

The weekend ended rapidly and I found it heartbreaking to see Gwyn and Courtney board the Amtrak. We all hugged each other and I found it hard to let Gwyn go. I knew it would be awhile before I would see her again. It all seemed a blur as I watched the train pull out. I felt like I was caught up in a movie that leads the viewer to buy into the next sequel.

Me, Mom, Delia (Gwyn's adoptive mom), and Gwyn

Mother's Day 2009 Marvin, Ethan, Rosa, me, Tommy,
Mom, Gwyn, Lisa, and James

Since our reunion, we have managed to have several more annual reunions together. With Tommy and his fiancée Marvat living in Alaska, Gwyn and her family living in Colorado, and Lisa's family and James living in Oregon, getting together has been a challenge. Nonetheless, we have managed to have the some of the best times that a family could possibly have. We have bonded and have come closer than most brothers and sisters can be.

2009 Family Reunion at Mom's house. Gwyn, Tommy
and w/Ethan, me, Lisa, and James

From left to right: Jackson (Gwyn's son), Moose and fiancé,
me with Lisa behind me.

Gwyn to my left, Tommy with Ethan (Lisa's son) on his
shoulders. Marvat (Tommy's fiancé), Lauren (Gwyn's daughter),
Eric (Lisa's husband), Mike (Gwyn's ex husband)

White river rafting with family in Sunriver Resort, OR

All 5 siblings on the final day of our 2013 Sunriver reunion.
Lisa, Tommy, James, Tony & Gwyn

11

Epilogue

I HAVE CARRIED THE scar of this emotional abuse for several decades and have not allowed it to heal. I now realize that this wound needs to be bandaged and mended. It won't come from the long desired I'm sorry from my abusive adoptive parents. That's not possible nor is it reality. After therapy (yes, successful) and reading The Five People You Meet in Heaven by Mitch Albom, I believe it all comes down to forgiving others, forgiving yourself, and accepting that everything happens for a reason. For some that may be a hard pill to swallow, but in the end, perhaps the reason for me to experience this is so I could help others.

Would I be where I am in my life today if I wasn't adopted, and my horrible ordeal had never happened? With this book, will I indirectly impact someone else's life for the better?

I won't know the answers to these questions until I pass to the other side. What I do know is that hatred is an extremely negative feeling to have or to carry around with you for any period of time. It will weigh you down emotionally and spiritually to the point that it can manifest itself physically and take its toll on your health and well-being.

In closing, my story mirrors the stories of millions of others. However, the cycle of child abuse can be broken. It all starts with you. You can make a difference in the life of a child and like the movie mentioned above, that impact will carry forward in their lives and impact the lives of everyone with whom they come in contact. One small positive action will become a domino effect that multiplies a hundred fold. Whether you are a coach, teacher, or next door neighbor, one small validation can go a very long way in a child's life. If they are unable to thank you now, I thank you on their behalf. I also thank you for taking the time to read my story. I hope that it has made a difference in your life in how you will positively impact others; directly or indirectly.

12

The Unexpected Chapter

PRIOR TO THIS chapter I thought I had completed documenting this journey. However, as life goes on, so do the chapters. Even with death, the chapters still continue. Such is the cycle of life.

As I sit in my adoptive parents' living room, for some ironic reason I choose tonight to select the record button to transcribe my thoughts and memories again. I look at the date and today is December 18, 2014. My adoptive mother would have been 80 years old on this day; her birthday.

I press the rewind button now and it takes me back a few months ago to approximately September 15, 2014. I'm looking in the guest bathroom mirror of my parent's house, and I realize it's almost 36 years since I looked at this very mirror. The last time I looked, the reflection was that of a 14-year-old young boy who was punched in the face several times by his mother and then told to go look in the mirror, so he could see how ugly he truly was. I promised to never return to this very mirror once I was old enough to leave this godforsaken nightmare. It was a face filled with hatred, sadness, terror, and disbelief of what I was going through.

Looking into the mirror now, I see past my own reflection and still see that 14-year-old boy looking back. That boy has become a man that no longer holds the hatred that was the core of his existence. As I

MOMMY? NO!!

walked out of the bathroom and to the left, I looked down at what was once an old worn-out hallway carpet that has been replace by a cherry wood floor. Just a few steps away and immediately to my right was once my bedroom. My old bed, dresser, study desk, record player, and 1979 Dodgers pennant that was once on the wall, are no longer there. In place of all those items, are bags filled with saline solution bottles, adult diapers, bathing sponges, and various other healthcare equipment and supplies.

At the end of the hallway is the spare bedroom that once held all my father's stereo equipment and vinyl records from the 50s and 60s. This was his getaway room, or 'man cave' as we call it today. This was a room that he would play his Nat King Cole, Andy Williams, Frank Sinatra, the Four Seasons, and Tony Bennett records; to name just a few. Very much the way I collected, categorized, and maintained my baseball cards was the way he managed his vinyl records. The only thing left in the room was a queen-size bed and my old dresser. Before I had to move my mom to a care facility, the caretaker slept in this room during the last days my mom was living in the house.

All that is left in the living room is an old Italian leather couch and recliner which could not be sold at the estate sale. Against the left wall are two large wooden, sliding glass shelves that once contained my mother's precious handmade Japanese kimono dolls. At the furthest wall an old hand carved Japanese china cabinet still stands exactly where it was thirty four years ago. It once housed all of my mother's prized china plates, crystal glasses, stainless steel 'holiday only cutlery', and other special 'look but don't touch' treasures. In her eyes, these items were priceless and represented wealth. At long last, they were sold for pennies on the dollar. This made it very clear to me what the difference was between intrinsic and extrinsic value. It also underscored the old adage of "you can't take it with you". For these reasons, I knew I could not be present during the estate sale. I couldn't bear to see these priceless items that my parents held so true to their heart, become devalued in a world that treated them as insignificant. However, that's the cold, hard reality of it.

DAD PASSES AWAY

I hit the rewind button in my mind again. The date is May 20, 2014. When I saw the certified letter from my cousin, I didn't expect what I read. It was dated May 2, 2014 and contained three lines:

Tony, this is your cousin Sergio. I am sorry to tell you that your dad passed away on Sunday, April 13, 2014. Your mom's condition is not the best and is bed ridden. Give me a call when you get a chance.

I sat in my car in a complete stupor. I kept reading those three lines over and over again. My body and mind began to feel as if it was all going numb. I just kept saying "No. No! No...dad. Dad!?" It was all I could say to myself. This couldn't be true. This wasn't supposed to happen like this! This is not how I saw his ending. This is not how I planned for him to die! This ...wasn't... how...it...was...supposed...to...

I was in a comatose state. I don't know how long I sat in my car that night. Finally when I got myself together, I called Sergio. He said that my dad had complications from a lung surgery and died in his sleep. There was much more detail than that but it was all I heard and could comprehend. He asked if I could come home to take care of all the paperwork. He said that they couldn't cremate my dad without a next of kin signature and my mom was not capable. I immediately went into overdrive and began to think how long it would take me to drive from Sacramento to Los Angeles. It was 6:30pm and it would be about a 7 hour drive. I wouldn't be able to do anything tonight so in my best interest I waited until the early morning.

This isn't how I envisioned this life journey would end. I always thought my mother would pass before my father. Then my dad and I could continue the relationship where it had left off many years ago when mom was hospitalized. I had so many things to talk about, so many things I wanted to do with him. I wanted to hear about his tours in Vietnam and Korea. I wanted to bond with my dad again. I wanted to tell him that despite how much he defended my mom, that I still loved him. There were baseball games, boxing, Monday night football and beers to drink. I wanted to tell him of all my accomplishments and all the ones I still had to accomplish.

I wanted to hear him say 'Good job, son. I'm really proud of you.' It was too late now. None of these things could happen now. Due to my stubbornness and my inability to forgive and forget, I would now live the rest of my life in regret. It wasn't supposed to happen like this...it just wasn't supposed to...

REUNIFICATION PART II

I pulled into Los Angeles about 3pm the next day. It was a step back in time. The hamburger joint was still in business on the two main cross streets leading into my old neighborhood. The houses where I used to mow the lawns for $5.00 looked just like I remembered it back in 1980. I pulled onto my street and reduced my speed down to a slow roll. My anxiety level elevated and breathing seemed to be an added effort. The house looked like it had a new coat of paint and the lawn was well manicured. There was a car in the driveway that I didn't recognize. I parked and got out of the car. I took a deep breath not knowing what to expect. As I began to knock on the metal, white, security screen door, a man came out dressed in scrubs, backpack, and a clipboard. I introduced myself and he greeted me as the nurse from hospice to do a medical assessment of my mom. As he began to update me, another man came walking up the driveway. He was short and somewhat diminutive in stature but dressed in slacks and a sport coat. As he got closer, he extended his hand with a big smile and realizing that I didn't recognize him, he said "Tony? It's me Sergio!"

Sergio was always the big cousin that I had admired when I was just a young boy. He was the big brother that I always wanted to be like. I remembered him as being tall, confident, athletic, and intelligent. After all, he was heading to USC and would be the first in the family to graduate from college. His little brothers and I use to try to gang up on him and attempt to wrestle him to the ground to no avail. I was ten years old back then. Time had altered us both physically and I felt like I towered over him. Sergio had aged and it occurred to me that I, too, must look different to him. When he looked up at me, he hugged me and said "How's it goin' big guy!?" I responded that I'd be better if we were meeting under different circumstances but it was good to see him nonetheless. He said he was sorry about my dad but now he needed to prepare me with what was immediately at hand. We turned to the hospice nurse and he began to give me a rundown of my mom's medical condition.

"Your mom is doing well. Her BP and other vitals are normal. Based on my assessment, your mom no longer qualifies for hospice care. Here's my card, in case you have any questions or need any further assistance."

I wasn't sure how to respond to what he just said, but it appeared that this was good news. I took his card, thanked him and told him I would call him if I had any questions. As he walked away, I looked at Sergio to get his read on the nurse's assessment but he appeared unaffected. He told me to prepare myself for what I was about to see. He explained that my mom wouldn't look the same as I had last seen her. He went on to say that she had extreme weight loss and has been bedridden for quite a while. She needed 24 hour care and couldn't feed or take care of herself due to severe dementia. He paused and calmly said she may not recognize me. Outside of my dad, she had not recognized anyone in several months and oftentimes wouldn't recognize my dad. Just when I thought I heard the worst, he added that my mom also had lost her left leg as a result of MRSA[16]. Her doctor had to immediately amputate her leg from just above the knee to stop the MRSA from spreading through the rest of her body.

I wasn't prepared for this. I felt my body and mind go numb. I was on overload already and I felt this was the final stone that would collapse the pillars that held up the foundations of my soul. With Sergio's hand on my back to steady me, I walked into the house and to the master bedroom where my mom was. I paused at the doorway for a moment and took a deep breath. As I walked into the room, I saw a very

---

16 **Methicillin-resistant *Staphylococcus aureus*** is a bacterium responsible for several difficult-to-treat infections in humans. Also commonly referred to as flesh eating bacteria.

small, frail person lying on a hospital bed. Her right leg was completely flexed up and bent at the knee and there was a small stump where her left leg used to be. It appeared as though there was only half a person in front of me. For a brief moment she looked right through me as if I didn't even exist. And then immediately after, her eyes seemed to glow with happiness and gave me the biggest smile I had ever seen in my life. She grunted happily and I could tell she knew who I was. I quickly walked over to her bedside and gave her the longest and biggest hug I've ever given her.

"Hi Mom! How are you? You okay? I'm here now. Everything will be okay. You have nothing to worry about!"

She kept looking up at me with a smile that I had never seen before. It was the first time in my life that I felt she was genuinely happy to see me. She tried to talk but I couldn't comprehend everything she was trying to say, but it was evident that she was overjoyed at my presence. She kept touching my arm and saying how handsome I was in Japanese. She wouldn't let go and the feeling of validation and acknowledgment was overwhelming. I had never felt this type of recognition and love from her in all my life until this very moment.

I'm not sure how long that moment lasted but I wanted it to last forever. I tried to pull away from her for a moment to talk to Sergio but she gave me a look of 'Please don't go.' I told her I would be right back and that it would only take a moment. She seemed to understand and gave me a smile.

Sergio was waiting in the hallway and I could tell he had been holding back tears. He said it was the first time in a long time that she reacted to anyone in the way she just did, never mind the fact the she actually recognized me.

"That was a miracle! She hasn't smiled or lit up like that in a very, very long time 'Cuz'! That was awesome!"

He suggested we go out and have lunch and get caught up as well as give me a bunch of legal documents that I needed to take over.

Over the next few months, I became the care taker for my mom. During that time, it was discovered that a bone was protruding from my mom's skin at the amputation point. The hospice doctor said that it was normal due to the atrophy of the leg muscle and recommended another amputation. Without it, there would be the possibility of an infection. However, the amputation didn't come without its own risk. Mom's health was failing and going under anesthesia was risky. I asked the doctor what was the worst case scenario if the bone was left protruding from the stump. He said there was a greater risk of infection and mom could die of sepsis.

Mom's surgery went well and from there she was admitted to an assisted living center. Sadly, it was minimal; just a bed and a desk with a curtain separating her from her roommate. I felt major guilt in leaving her there. I had no choice since I couldn't provide the care and medication she needed. I sat on the edge of her bed, held her hand and apologized to her over and over again. She just looked at me and smiled, oblivious to her new barren surroundings. She was just happy that I was with her. I waited until she fell asleep that night and cried on the drive home. It was all too overwhelming for me. Her life and well-being all depended on whatever decisions I made on her behalf. It was a huge load to shoulder.

I worked in Sacramento and she was in San Gabriel Valley. It was a seven hour drive and I visited her as often as I could. In my mind it wasn't enough and compounded the guilt. I felt I needed to be by her side 24/7 but it wasn't financially feasible. After three weeks, I came back and she was thriving. She was able to be in a wheelchair and sit straight up on her own. Prior to this, she was bedridden for over a year. Adding to this, she had gained 7 pounds! This was a huge milestone!

I brought pictures of my dad and her family. She was able to recognize my dad and said "That's my viejo[17]! He's a good man!" That was amazing and spoke volumes. My dad loved my mom to the very end; to the point that it killed him.

---

17 Endearing term in Spanish for *husband*.

Eight Years Unfolded

In the few months that I was at my parents' house, I had to go through all their personal effects, documents, and finances. As I went through my parent's piles of medical documentation, the missing chapters of the last eight years began to unfold like a mystery novel. They both had suffered physically, mentally, financially, and emotionally to extreme degrees. With the onset of my mom's dementia, began an emotional tailspin for my dad. Mom became even more aggressive, violent, and verbally abusive towards my dad. Mom had twisted her knee on one of her daily walks which then required a meniscus repair. That then led to the amputation of her left leg. Soon after she became completely dependent on my dad for all her needs.

My dad's career in the military and U.S. Post Office began to catch up to him. He had several surgeries to his shoulder from years of carrying the mailbags. He also had repeated surgeries on his knees as a result of a dog that attacked him which caused a severe meniscus tear much like my mom's. Eventually his heart would began to give out resulting in triple bypass surgery. This then led to an infection in his lung and ultimately took his life. However, it wasn't the infection that killed him, it was his desire to be with my mom at her bedside when he thought she would soon pass away. The true reason for his death was based on what I was about to uncover.

As I sifted through the myriad of files filled with copies of medical records, I found hospice documentation that indicated that mom had only six months to live. It was dated January 2014. This month was May, which meant mom only had a month to live! I called the hospice immediately. When I called, I was in a complete panic. My anxiety hit an all-time high and I felt myself begin to emotionally unravel. This was rapidly becoming a double barreled shotgun blast to my soul.

The nurse that took my call had been working on my mom's case from day one. She could hear and sense the stress in my voice. She had to do all she could to calm me down on the phone. It wasn't until she told me that off the record, "this was just a paperwork process" that was done in order to get her qualified for in home hospice care. It didn't mean that

TONY LADRON DE GUEVARA JR

she actually only had six months to live. It was the only way she could receive the hospice care she needed. With dementia, there really was no way to determine just how much time she had left. While I was relieved to hear that, it began to slowly dawn on me that my dad had no way of knowing this information.

It was in January of 2014 that my dad had to go in for his heart by-pass surgery. I don't know if receiving mom's hospice paperwork was the cause of his heart condition. Whether it was romantic irony or not, the final result was tragic. If he had known that mom's prognosis was just made up, he could very well be alive today.

Soon after his surgery, dad came home for a short period and then was quickly readmitted for a lung infection and another surgery. They had to remove the lower lobe of his lung and that required him to be on an oxygen machine while hospitalized as an inpatient. He was there for months but with June looming around the corner; he decided he wanted to come home to be with my mom.

Based on the hospice document, I can only speculate that my father calculated that mom only had a couple of months to live. He had spent too much time in the hospital and not enough time at home taking care of and being with her. He had hired a friend to administer to mom's needs and care on a 24x7 basis, but he wanted to be with her no matter what; even if it killed him. And he did exactly that. On April 10, 2014, dad signed the legal paperwork to leave AMA (against medical advice). Three days later, he passed away in his bed at home where mom was.

THE EPIPHANY

Upon returning home after being informed that my dad had passed, I spent the next four months at my mom's bedside as much as I possibly could. I brought her pictures from when she was a teenager until the most current pictures I could find. She would recognize most everyone in the pictures but in time, the only one she would recognize was her 'viejo'.

Whenever I showed up, she would light up like a Christmas tree. It then occurred to me why she had never reacted to me like this before. It was actually all too simple. The dementia had wiped her memory clean. It was as if she had an ECT[18]. She couldn't remember all the tragedy that occurred in her life. Therefore, without all those memories to influence her behavior, her emotions and reactions were based on the here and now! She no longer had the horrible memories that caused her to be abusive toward me. What I was experiencing for the first time in my life, was she now viewed me through the eyes of a loving mom. She no longer hated me based on her bad childhood memories!

This epiphany caused me to become a kid again. I wanted to do everything I could to make her happy. I would bring her all her favorite foods and desserts. I would show her "YouTube" videos of sumo wrestling matches that I knew she loved. She smiled and laughed and I could tell she enjoyed all the things I brought or showed her. In the short time we had together, we made up for 50 years of mother and son bonding! It was an incredible feeling of joy, validation, and love that I had never experienced with her in all my life. That, however, would all come to an abrupt end.

In the last weeks of September of 2013, mom's condition slowly deteriorated to the point that she became a scared tortoise in a shell. She no longer responded to me and soon thereafter, she would just stare past me. For me, this was worse than if she had already passed on.

I began to question life and divinity. Was this God's way of making us pay for our sins? Was this purgatory? Why would a forgiving God cause someone to suffer this way? I told God that I forgave mom and there was no reason for her to suffer anymore. I told mom that if this was her way of holding on to make sure I was okay; I told her I'd be fine. I let her know that I truly forgave her for how she treated me and that I understood it

---

18 Electroconvulsive therapy (ECT), formerly known as electroshock therapy and often referred to as shock treatment, is a standard psychiatric treatment in which seizures are electrically induced in patients to provide relief from psychiatric illnesses.

was her own tragic upbringing that caused her to become who she was. She no longer was that person at this moment and for the first time, I could see and experience the pure and loving mom that she truly was. I let her know that if she was holding on because she needed forgiveness from me or God, then it was granted. I no longer wanted her to suffer and if there was any penance to pay, it was overpaid.

On September 24th, mom became feverish. When I got to her bedside, she was not responsive to my touch or my voice. She was completely catatonic and could just make gurgling sounds. After antibiotics were administered, she improved over the next few days but no longer could eat and was on IV's for fluid. She was shutting down physically and finally on October 1st, while on my way to see her, I received the call. The hospice nurse said he was sorry for my loss and my mom had just passed. I was caught in Los Angeles midtown traffic and only 9 minutes away.

When I got to her bedside, I sat next to her and put my hand on top of hers. I told her again that I forgave her and to say hi to dad. I didn't cry like I thought I would. I actually felt relief that mom was no longer suffering. She was no longer physically here but I felt her presence in the room listening to me. I never imagined how this day would be but it wasn't anything like this. I never thought I would forgive my mom for what she did to me, but I did. In the last few months that I was with her, I experienced my true mom; she loved holding my hand, she missed me when I had to leave, she was proud of me and was always happy to see me. Most important of all, she did, in fact, love me.

Poem: A Child of Five

Void of emotion
Not able to care
Clutching his tear drenched
One eyed teddy bear
Facing the corner
On his bare knees
Six hours punished
For not saying "please"
He sits and waits
Plays in his imaginary zoo
Daddy will be home soon
And he will beat him too
Cuts and bruises
Bumps and welts
From broom handles, fists
Sticks and belts
He can't perceive
This total insanity
That fills his ears daily
With frenzied profanity
Why do they torture
And constantly deprive
He is only a child
A child of five

Tony Ladron de Guevara, Jr.

CODA

It's been just over a year since my mother passed. Even with the understanding of why she treated me the way she did, I rarely think about her unless I run across an archived picture of her on my cell phone. I keep both of my parent's ashes in miniature urns in my living room but admittedly they don't invoke any emotion when I look at them. I try to put some logic to this uncaring callousness but I come up with nothing.

On October 1st of this month (2015), I woke up finding myself kicking violently at the covers at the foot of the bed. My heart was rapidly beating and my breathing labored. I was drenched in sweat. I had a nightmare that my dad was beating me and trying to pull me to the ground while I was viciously kicking his head in self-defense.

The following night, I woke up in the same physical state. This time I woke up while delivering high, overhead, haymaker punches to the other side of the bed. This time it was my mom that I was fending off. The nightmare was real. What I mean by that is I felt her presence. It was a physical presence that I cannot find the words to explain.

Both of these incidents were extremely disquieting to me. As I tried to retrace the events of the preceding day, I couldn't pinpoint a situation, a memory, or even a thought that could have possibly triggered those very physical dreams.

And then it hit me like a runaway bullet train! It was the anniversary of my mom's passing. But why these unsettling dreams? Why were they so real to me? Is this what Post Traumatic Stress Disorder is all about? Or was it something more surreal? Maybe both. The dreams stopped after the second incident. I'm hoping they don't return. I had hoped for closure.

I keep the military police baton that my mom beat me with on the floor of my kitchen between the refrigerator and the cabinets. I made myself think I'd need it for protection one day in case of an intruder. But on a subconscious level, I am not wanting to let go of that memory and I can't explain that either.

It's obvious to me that I need a complete spiritual and emotional cleansing. Along with burning that baton, it's time to take the ashes from that along with my parent's ashes and scatter them to the sea. I need to let this be the final chapter and I feel this is the way to do it.

October 23, 2015

The day turned out to be something right out the storybook ending. It seemed almost too perfect in how all the elements of the clouds, sun, and wind came together. It was approximately 5 PM as dark clouds were making their way into the windy San Francisco Bay. However, the clouds ended just above the skyline. It was just a matter of time before the sun would appear as the clouds blew over the Golden Gate Bridge.

I made it to the midpoint of the bridge and looked over the railing. Under the bridge a freighter was lumbering through with its huge over-loaded cargo. As it made its way out to the open sea, the symbolism of this ship seemed befitting. It epitomized the pain that I've carried all these years in my heart. Now I watched as it made its way to an unknown destination. I knew I would never see that ship again.

On the previous night, I took a hacksaw and cut the baton in half. I found an old cooking pot and placed small pieces of wood at the bottom of the pot and soaked them and the baton with lighter fluid. I watched this weapon that was once used to beat me into submission, turn into a pile of harmless white ashes. Once the embers had calmed down, I placed those ashes in a sandwich bag.

Baton Burning Ceremony

I removed Mom and Dad's ashes from their miniature urns and wrapped tissue around the small plastic bags that their ashes were in.

I then placed them on the railings next to each other their urns and took a moment of silence to think about what this final milestone would represent.

Afterwards I took both urns and tossed them as far out from the bridge as I could and watched them hit the water. I then took each of their wrapped ashes and poked a hole through the tissue and the plastic bags. I threw my mother's ashes first, and watched a wispy trail of ashes come out of the bag as it made its way to the ocean below. I did the same with my dad's and watched his ashes fall to the sea as well. Finally, I took the sandwich bag that had the ashes of the baton, got on my knees and stretched my arm past the walkway deck and shook the bag to scatter the ashes. I didn't want those ashes to fly back up on to me. They represented evil to me and I didn't want any of it to ever touch me again.

Mom and Dad's ashes on the SF Bay Bridge

I stepped back for a moment and took a deep breath and let it out. I noticed that the cargo ship became a small speck on the huge ocean canvas. At that point, I tried to take a pulse read on what I was feeling; I got nothing. There wasn't a feeling of emotional closure that I had expected, but I felt that this chapter of my life had ended. I came to realize that the wound has healed, but the scar will always remain. And just like any other wounded warrior, I will share now my story with others to hopefully prevent them from becoming wounded as well.

The following sayings have been stated time and time again to the point of being cliché; however, these are the things for which I believe to be true and have helped me to survive and be where I am today -

1. *There is light at the end of every dark passageway.*
2. *You must persevere and believe that no matter what obstacles you face or cannot see, you can and will overcome them.*
3. *Read and be inspired about people who have succeeded from having nothing and/or recovered from tragedy.*
4. *Do unselfish things for people with no expectation of receiving anything in return.*
5. *You are the average of the five people closest to you. If you are not where you want to be in your life; reconsider the company you keep.*
6. *You control your thoughts; don't let negative thoughts control you.*
7. *Think and stay positive.*
8. *Be awesome, and never, ever give up!*

About the Author

Tony currently serves as the Director of a Sacramento, CA based consulting company. His first consulting contract for the Children at Risk Program under Department of Social Services put him in the midst of Social Worker trainees who urged him to tell and write his story. Since then, Tony is also a keynote and motivational speaker where he shares how, in the face of adversity, anything can be overcome.

For additional information on this author, go to;
   www.adoptedandabused.com